D

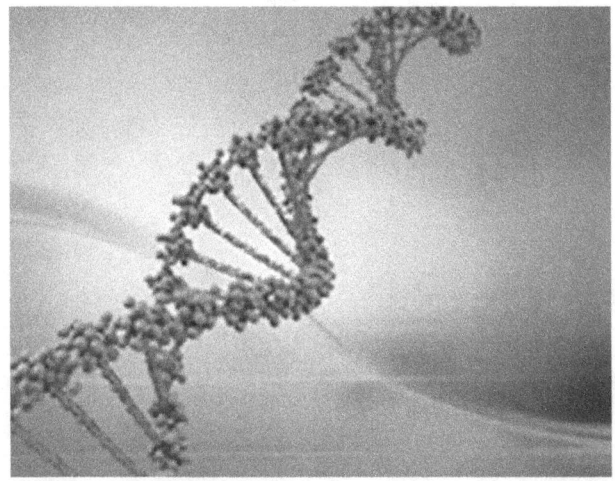

HARDWIRED...

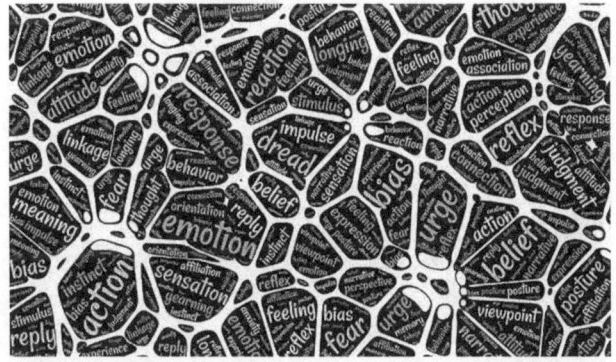

A Pocket Guide on Common Sense

James Knuckles

Copyright © 2023 James Knuckles
All rights reserved
First Edition

PAGE PUBLISHING
Conneaut Lake, PA

First originally published by Page Publishing 2023

ISBN 979-8-88793-866-0 (pbk)
ISBN 979-8-88793-868-4 (digital)

Printed in the United States of America

*To our son, Brien…handsome, smart, funny, loved to read…
We love and miss you, son!*

CONTENTS

Introduction xi

I.	Philosophy 1
II.	Common Sense Origins 39
III.	Perception or Belief versus Reality 41
IV.	Intelligence 53
V.	Ignorance 56
VI.	Mental Illness/Mental Health Disorders 58
VII.	Feelings 63
VIII.	Religion 69
IX.	Politics 75
X.	Racism 81
XI.	Relationships 91
XII.	Communication 98
XIII.	Parenting 103
XIV.	Humanity… "Don't Stop Your Human… Embrace It!"® 106
XV.	Life 113
XVI.	Values 118
XVII.	Money/Finances 125
XVIII.	Everyday Violators of the Rules of Common Sense 127
XIX.	Life's Lessons… Shitty Thoughts 135

Closing Thoughts 139

NOTE: There will be some social media posts in italics inserted in some chapters that are applicable throughout the book. The posts are from a weekly discussion group on a major social platform.

*I will not help you the way you want me to
help you… Your way is not working!*

—James Knuckles, circa July 2, 2021

INTRODUCTION

For many years, I have wondered why so many of us do some of the things we do that just don't seem to make very much common sense many times! It seemed to violate many of the commonsense rules or laws as I saw it! I began to wonder if I had a good grasp of the definition or meaning of common sense myself or if I even possessed it! Therefore, I decided to conduct some research on my own on some of the definitions and descriptions of common sense and discovered the following:

Sense:

- Sound practical intelligence
- A mental judgment, realization, or recognition
- Clear and sound mental faculties; sanity

Common:

- Occurring, found, or done often; prevalent
- Shared by, coming from, or done by more than one

Common sense:

- Good sense and sound judgment in practical matters
- The basic level of practical knowledge and judgment that we all need to help us live in a reasonable and safe way.
- Sound practical judgment that is independent of specialized knowledge, training, or the like; average native intelligence

- Our natural ability to make sound judgments and behave in a practical and sensible way
- Sound practical judgment concerning everyday matters or an essential ability to perceive, understand, and judge things that are shared by most others
- Common knowledge that most people, except babies and those with mental challenges, should know and possess (my favorite definition)

After thoroughly researching some of the most common definitions and descriptions of common sense, I concluded that I was definitely on the right track with my thoughts and beliefs about it and that I indeed possessed it! I feel the need at this point to note, nowhere in the definitions above or any other definitions or descriptions I have found, was there a mention of God, race, religion, faith, beliefs, gender, politics, etc., or any other thoughts that weren't based in fact, science, logic, or just plain common sense! So if we had to guess or choose what should influence or affect our daily lives more in a practical manner—God, religion, faith, beliefs, gender, race, and politics *or* facts, science, logic, and plain common sense—what would you choose? In my mind, your choice will indicate how much control and stability you believe you have in your life!

PHILOSOPHY

Please bear with me for a few minutes while I get somewhat technical for the purposes of understanding the terms which are the foundation of this book...

DNA: The genetic code that determines primarily the physiological characteristics of a living thing. Deoxyribonucleic acid, the technical name, is a self-replicating material present in nearly all living organisms as the main constituent of chromosomes; a threadlike structure of nucleic acids and protein found in the nucleus of most living cells, carrying genetic information in the form of genes. I like to think of it as primarily the "physical" part of our makeup that helps make us who we are physically, i.e., eye color, hair color, height, skin color, etc. Not much we can do about changing that part of our makeup as a living being other than some medical procedure possibly, and that only changes the physical appearance, not the actual DNA structure itself.

Hardwired: Genetically or innately determined, pertaining to or being a deep-rooted and relatively unmodifiable behavior or thought pattern in most cases. I like to think of this as the "psychological, mental, or emotional" part of our makeup or being that helps make us who we are from an attitudinal, thought, and behavior place. I strongly suspect this is why we as human beings have a problem with common sense most of the time. Through my research, I have not been able to find or see any other possible reason, other than for babies and those with mental challenges, for our complete lack of intelligence or common sense in many instances! For example, if I asked you what your favorite and least favorite colors were, could you tell me? I suspect you could. If I offered you $1,000,000 to change your most favorite color to your least favorite color and your least favorite color to your most favorite color, could you immediately do so on demand? I don't mean could you *tell* me you did it, but could you actually immediately intellectualize and internally *change* how you truly feel about the colors simply based upon a request in exchange for a large sum of money? I suspect you could not. If we can't consciously change our thoughts or behavior in life on something as simple and unimportant as our most favorite or least favorite colors on request or demand for a large sum of money, how can we change other more difficult and impactful aspects of our thoughts or life like race, religion, or politics for free? This is an example of being hardwired.

Common sense: Knowledgeable, sound, and prudent judgment based on a simple perception of the situation or facts shared by *nearly all* people *except* babies and those with mental challenges!

I suspect the people who don't fall into the babies, those with mental challenges, and nearly all categories referenced above are the group that causes us the most frustration and confusion. I like to call this group the other! This is the group I hope to get a better understanding of. I am very aware that we have certain beliefs or practices in our day-to-day lives that are in direct conflict with common sense! Race, politics, and religion are probably three of the biggest and most common violators of commonsense rules or principles! Yet those are the three topics many people are frequently heard saying, "If you don't want to lose or ruin good relationships, do not discuss race, politics, or religion!" The three topics that probably have the most impact on our daily lives and many feel and believe we should not discuss them! This is just one of many instances that just doesn't seem to make very much common sense to me!

Is our race determined by our DNA? Yes! Is our religion or our politics determined by our DNA? No, it is not! We can change our thoughts on religion or politics at any given time, and we often sometimes do, but we can't change our race! Are we hardwired one way or the other in our religious or political thoughts and beliefs? Even though I believe we can change our thoughts and beliefs on those things, it seems to me they are a lot harder to change when we are hardwired into a particular way of thinking!

I am very aware that this book will probably not change or affect most or practically any people's belief in their religion, politics, or any other major part of their life in a meaningful way due to them being hardwired one way or the other! So what is my goal or the point in writing this book if I don't believe it will change many or anyone's mind in a meaningful way? It has to do with my own, and hopefully many others' desire for understanding and finding clarity on the subject of common sense and why many of us act and behave the way we do many times! This is my opportunity to organize my own and others' thoughts on the subject of common sense I have had for many years on paper in a logical order and to bring a sense of clarity to myself and hopefully many others on something that I and many others see so clearly but many seem to have a problem grasping! It will also be an opportunity for enlightenment for so many who have told me they have had the same confusion with why so many seemingly smart and intelligent people they know and have known seem to have such a hard time grasping the concept of common sense in a meaningful way in so many cases! I am sure at one time or another all of us have had our common sense questioned by others. At this time, I would like you to take a moment and think of an area of your life where you have not been applying some general rules of common sense, and by the end of reading this book, start making a change! Hopefully after reading this book, depending on the outcome of your efforts to change, you will have a better understanding of the complexity and difficulty in consistently applying the rules of common sense on some issues or situations in our lives 100 percent of the time!

In December 2019, the coronavirus disease (COVID-19) was first reported in Wuhan, China. The first case in the United States was reported in January 2020. In March 2020, it was declared a worldwide pandemic (a disease that is prevalent over a whole country or the world). As of June 26, 2020, the reported worldwide cases were 9,473,214 and 484,249 deaths and still climbing! Worldwide governments, including the United States, had shut down their economies; to include, their educational systems, religious organizations, medical facilities were severely impacted; airline and transportation industries, in general, were decimated! There were hundreds of thousands of reported deaths worldwide as a result of the virus! These were all facts acknowledged by all the countries of the world and most of their people! Confronted with all these facts and much more, there were still many people, primarily in the United States and along political party lines, who believed the virus claim was a hoax or a conspiracy! Common sense-wise, they must have also believed this was a worldwide conspiracy where all of the world's countries and their people had gotten together to perpetrate this hoax! When asked why all the world's countries and people would do this, they didn't have a reasonable explanation for their thoughts and feelings other than they believed the hoax was perpetrated by the media and the Democratic Party, and that's just what they thought and believed! Many times, they would not discuss their reasoning and would get angry and refuse to continue discussing the subject! Common sense-wise, this thought pattern just doesn't make much common sense! Like with the favorite color analogy, it seems many of us are hardwired on our views about Covid-19 and find it equally difficult to change our feelings and thoughts on it, even though common sense wise, it doesn't make much sense to think that the whole world is involved in such a large and elaborate scheme and conspiracy! What is the purpose of this elaborate hoax? What's the payoff for the people of the world perpetrating the hoax?

In December 2020, the first vaccine for COVID-19 was released for public use. Approximately 45 percent of Americans refused to take the vaccine for many various reasons, mostly political. It was determined by the medical and scientific communities that at least 90 percent of those who took the vaccine for COVID-19 would not contact COVID-19. Of the remaining 10 percent who may have contacted COVID-19 while having taken the vaccine, the majority would not get sick enough to have to be hospitalized. In the small percent that may have to be hospitalized, none would die. At this time, in January 2022, even after being made aware of these statistics and facts, approximately 45 percent of Americans still refused to take the vaccine.

> *And now you are dead…*
> *I just spoke to you a few months ago. I suggested to you that you get the shot; you said no, you would not…and now you are dead…*

DNA... HARDWIRED...

We all will have to go one day, but did you have to go that way...before your time, some will say. I still ask myself why. I too don't think it was your time to die...

A virus took you away when there was a vaccine, you could have taken to save the day... We all have a choice; we all have a voice... You let others' voice make your choice...

Some say it was politics; some say it was the side effects of getting sick. Doesn't matter...it is all just unreasonable chatter...

If you were alive today, would you be so reckless and do it the same way...

Your family and friends will miss you dearly. Hopefully they will see what happened to you clearly... They too have a voice... Will they also allow others to make their choice...

Many like you were asked to take the shot, and like you, they said they would not, and like you, now they are dead...

Some individuals and institutions were so committed in their resistance to the facts concerning COVID-19 that they were willing to do the following:

- Washington State University football coach, Nick Rolovich, and four of his assistants were fired for refusing to take the COVID-19 vaccine. He claimed a religious exemption from the mandate, but it was denied. He was earning $3.1 million per year.
- Brooklyn Nets NBA star, Kyrie Irving, was pulled from playing or even practicing with his team until he complied with the vaccine mandate. Each missed game would cost him $381,181.22.
- Many other professional athletes chose to lose money and their careers in many cases.

- Active-duty military members chose to be discharged rather than take the COVID-19 vaccine.
- Schoolteachers, police officers, medical professionals, etc. chose to be terminated rather than take the COVID-19 vaccine.
- Many people became seriously ill and/or died for refusing to take the COVID-19 vaccine.
- Many people witnessed these illnesses and deaths and still refused to take the COVID-19 vaccine.

Observation: It has been said that "it ain't so much people's ignorance that does the harm as their knowing so darned much that ain't so" (*Josh Billings*).

Observation: My oldest daughter, who was close to fifty years old at the time and a registered nurse, told me she had not taken a vaccine for COVID-19 after three vaccines had been available for use for approximately a year. All three vaccines were approved by the FDA under an emergency use authorization order. After our discussion, she decided to take one of the vaccines because she was a smart and sensible individual, and it just made sense! After a few days of taking the first of two shots, one of the other vaccines that she had not taken had become available under a normal FDA approval order. She contacted me and told me that she was now having second thoughts and regretted taking the shot! She implied that I may have guilted her into taking the shot even though she realized at the time, and even now, that taking the shot was the smart and right thing to do! What manner of reasoning, logic, intelligence, or common sense was at work here?

Note: There will be some social media posts in italics inserted in some chapters that are applicable throughout the book. The posts are from a weekly discussion group on common sense on a major social platform.

March 30, 2022 (social media post): *I am presently writing a book on common sense. Common sense simply put is "knowledge that should be common to most people except babies and the* mentally challenged!" I have been gathering information for my book from many sources. I have researched other writings on the subject, interviewed many people, observed day-to-day life and world events, and utilized my own personal experiences with common sense. The recent Will Smith and Chris Rock incident has provided me with even more confirmation that many of us have a lapse of common sense at times! If you haven't heard by now, Will Smith, the well-known actor who was up for his first Oscar, walked up on stage at the 2022 Oscars ceremony and smacked Chris Rock, the host of the Oscars, once in the face and walked off stage and took his seat. He continued the assault on Chris Rock by yelling some profanities at him from his seat! Please remember the definition of common sense: "knowledge that should be common to most people except babies and the mentally challenged!" I would expect that most people, except babies and the mentally challenged, would see this situation basically the same, but that is not what I am finding! Please note the following:

The world witnessed an act of physical and verbal assault and violence of one man against another with the following reactions:

o   The person attacked did not respond in kind.
o   No one intervened in the incident at the time.
o   The attacker was not arrested and was allowed to continue in the event.

o   *The attacker won and was given an Oscar at the event with a standing ovation and joyous applause.*

Comments and reactions I have seen and heard up to this point after the event:

o   *The attacker has not been arrested, and the person attacked declined to press charges.*
o   *It was agreed by most people, including the victim of the attack, that the joke made by the victim, which apparently prompted the attack, was cruel and very insensitive.*
o   *The attacked person has sincerely apologized to the attacker and his family for his role in the matter.*
o   *The attacker did eventually apologize to the attacked person after a day or two of the incident.*
o   *Many say that the violent attack was justified because of a "history" or "backstory" of the attacked individual making jokes about the attacker and his spouse.*
o   *Some say this was a show of a Black man's strong love and support for his wife, and they approved of his actions.*

So my thoughts on the incident and how common sense applies…or doesn't:

First I totally agree that Chris Rock's "joke" was very cruel and insensitive! Even he acknowledges that! I saw the look on Jada's face immediately after the joke, and I could see how deeply it hurt her! I don't know her, and it hurt me to see how deeply she was hurting! So, I can only imagine how deeply Will Smith was hurt and as a result his anger! I totally disagree with his taking the action he took!

Second some questions for the people who feel Will was justified with his reaction to Chris' comment...looking for yes or no answers:

1. *What if it was a White man who smacked Chris for the same situation and the consequences were the same, would you feel the same?*
2. *Do you believe Will Smith would have smacked Curtis James Jackson (50 cent) or Dwayne "The Rock" Johnson if they had told the same joke about Jada?*
3. *Do you think it was an assault and an act of violence?*
4. *Do you think it is okay to assault or commit an act of violence on someone because they verbally hurt your or a loved ones' feelings?*

Finally this is not a judgment but my continued search for answers and understanding in my pursuit of reasons why all people, other than babies and the mentally challenged, don't see common sense in the same way.

Response: FV: *1.) No, 2.) yes, 3.) yes, 4.) no. Okay, those were my answers to your question. Now my opinion of that event: As a comedian, Will found the joke funny, not insensitive. He laughed at; Jada didn't like it, and I'm going to assume provoked him in some form to do what he did. Common sense will tell you there is a time and place for everything, but the part of your brain that causes you to react without thinking will have you forget common sense and do dumb shit. I can't say how I would have responded in that situation, but in today's world where Black-on-Black violence is crazy but we mad about White-on-Black crime, that wouldn't be the time or place for me to act on that situation with violence—on national TV and in front of thousands of witnesses. Let's reverse the situation. If that was a woman comedian, would Jada have gone on stage and do the same thing, or would she still expect her husband to go take care of the situation the same way? Situations are never solved with violence; it only makes the matter worse, and at their age,* COMMON SENSE SHOULD HAVE KEPT HIS ASS FROM DOING WHAT HE DID AT THAT TIME. *Consequences for my action,* JAIL FINES RUIN MY CAREER WHICH IS MY MONEY *for a woman that I love but just had an entanglement with my son's friend in my damn house and justified her action, me still being in this marriage and trying to work it out is enough to show my love for you not smacking the taste out another man's moufffff for a joke that wasn't a joke. I for one would love to see Jada play GI Jane!*

My response: James Knuckles: *FV, thank you for your thoughtful and excellent responses! I greatly appreciate it! I am presently writing a book on common sense, and your responses are very helpful! You gave me some things to think about the situation I hadn't thought about! Thank you again!*

Response: MD: *I do not agree with Will Smith's actions; it could have been handled privately.*

My response: *MD, thank you! I had not thought about the option of Will talking to Chris privately...*

Response: MD: *Thanks, cuz.*

Response: FV: *And think about this angle, it could have been planned. Why a smack, not a punch!*

Response: MC: *Some people do things and don't think much about common sense sometimes. They get carried away about things that they can't control, and their emotion take over... It just happens sometimes that people react so quickly just on how they perceive things... It's my humble opinion about common sense... Thanks.*

My response: *Thank you, MC! You hit on a key point when you mentioned perception! Many times, we react based on our perceptions, and it may not make much sense to others because they don't perceive the situation the same way we do!*

Response: MC: *That's mostly what people do. We know how we react based on how we feel about this stuff. People act differently, and I guess it is normal as human beings... How's that?*

Response: GO: *I do not believe there is such a thing as common sense. There is common knowledge, i.e., hold an apple in your outstretched hand and release it. It will fall to the ground. Every human being all around the world learns this at some point. But our "senses" are unique and highly individualized. They are a result of our gender, our upbringing, our cultural background, and our environment, to name just a few. But I wish you well in your endeavor. Looking forward to see your conclusions.*

Response: JR: *Hollywood events ratings are going down, so they must do something to get individual attention. STAGED.*

My response: *Hey, JR! Thank you for your feedback! I have heard some people say that, but I personally don't know! If it was staged, I don't think it looked good for any of the parties involved, including Hollywood!*

Response: AWJ: *You're going to be writing a 1000-page novel! I'll read it.*

My response: *Lol! I am sure it will not be 1000 pages; I don't have that much to say or knowledge, but thanks for the confidence! Lol!*

Response: RC: *Great topic, Knuckles; my wife and I was discussing this the other day. I was trying to explain to her that the term "common sense" varies from person to person based on their experiences and environment. An individual perception is their reality, and I believe that this guides and shapes their common sense. I find myself questioning why more people are not exercising "common sense," then I remember this speech I heard Dave Chappelle give about "good or bad versus better or worse." Check it out, I think it will help explain a lot! Let me know if you can't find it, and I will try and send you the link.*

My response: *Hey, RC, thanks! All sounds great! You hit on some things I am covering in the book that many of us don't think about or consider when we are dealing with others in our day-to-day lives! Without going into all the things I will cover in the book, I just think there are many things in life that we should agree on no matter our backgrounds, like whether or not it is okay or not to smack some-*

one because they hurt our feelings or made us upset! I understand we are human, and we will get upset at times and let our feelings get the best of us, but again, after everything is said and done, we can't agree on whether or not it is okay or not to assault someone for hurting our feelings? Thanks again for your feedback, RC! I think the more we discuss this topic, the better we will be able to understand each other!*

Response: RC: *Knuckles, watch this and tell me what you think. https://youtu.be/-NN-KWdZBI4, Dave Chappelle at Allen University: "With great power comes great responsibility."*

My response: *RC, I watched the clip and felt it was inspiring! I think, and you can correct me if you disagree, but I think he was reflecting on some of his personal experiences and decisions in his life and how others may have viewed his decisions as not sensible. I think he was encouraging us to live our lives according to our values and ethics and not others' values and ethics! I agree! I truly believe as long we aren't hurting ourselves and others, we need to live our lives in a way that fulfills us and makes us happy...*

Response: FV: *Sometimes we are viewed or judged with not making sound decisions and those decisions are tied with common sense decisions but for you the person making the decision it made all the sense in the world (common sense will tell you to take the $50 million deal)*

Response: RC: *When it comes to our values and ethics, I believe he was saying that we use "better or worse" to guide our behavior instead of "good or bad," and by doing this, it has negatively affected our ethics and values or in reference to your topic, our "common sense." What do you think?*

My response: *I think better or worse is just another way of judging an action or decision when you aren't sure of the possible outcome at the time you make the decision, like getting married. Another example, Chappelle made the decision not to take the fifty million at the time not knowing if it was going to be for the better or worse. He was also judging whether it was going to be a good or bad decision for him. If you do some research on why he finally said he left, you will see that he was definitely going through some "life" issues at the time he made the decision. He can now look back at his decision and say it was for the better for him because he maintained his ethics and did a good thing and still made sixty million in the process later!*

Response: RC: *This is a GREAT topic; it shows us how people can take two different positions from the same statement! I agree that better or worse is another way of judging an action or decision, but we too often use that standard (better or worse) when making decisions because most times it's the easier choice. Dave addressed this when he said, "When we use better or worse, we are like a mouse in a maze searching for the cheese, but when we use 'good or bad,' we realize that we are in a maze..." I think he was saying that his decision to turn down the fifty million was a good decision, not a better decision. I could be wrong, but that's my take...or should I say "common sense..."*

DNA... HARDWIRED...

My response: *RC, I agree this is a great topic, and I want to thank you and others for adding to this learning experience! Yes, you are right! We are able to take a single subject or issue and have many people look at it and have different takes and opinions on it, and we can still all agree that it is okay that we each see it the way we do. For example, the glass is half empty or half full analogy. Some people see the glass as half full and others see it as half empty. Who is right? Why of course, they are both right, right? That is how I see Chappelle's analogy about the mouse, cheese, and the maze. Some people choose to use the terms good or bad and other people prefer to use the terms better or worse. I understand for him, and maybe for you, looking at his decision as good or bad brought him to the realization that he was like a mouse in a maze chasing the cheese. That's great! For me, either analogy will work. I think the key is that we get there no matter the impetus. I suspect most people, other than babies and the mentally challenged, might agree...*

Response: RC: *The good thing about all of this is that we have determined that we all have common sense...* 😊😄😆😺

Response: PBR: *I know I may not be popular with my comments but here they go. I have systemic lupus since eighty-one. I had to go through dialysis to try and save my kidneys. This in turn caused alopecia, lost three-fourth of all my hair. Losing your hair affects women more than men because we are judged by both men and women. It affected my family from my husband telling me when you see bald spots in public and my daughters getting into alter-*

cations at school when some child made a comment, made fun of me or about my hair. Will Smith lives with his wife, and he knows how an insensitive comment can hurt Jada. I'm personally happy to see him stand up to and slap Chris Rock. In older times, a slap was meant as an answer to an insult given to a gentleman or a gentleman's family.

My response: *Hello, PBR, and thanks for joining in on the conversation and sharing your personal story! I am sorry you have the illness you have and the consequences it has had on you and your family! I will in no way attempt to try and identify with what you and your family have gone through, try and minimize it, or try and tell you how you should feel and react to those feelings! As I have stated previously, I believe the joke Chris Rock told about Will's wife was totally cruel and insensitive and was inexcusable! I agree that in olden times, there were violent behaviors and norms that were accepted and approved of, like dueling to the death if you felt insulted, but thankfully today, we have progressed to a point where we settle our disputes in more of a civil manner. For example, today that slap could have cost Will a lot of money, ended his career, he could have ended up in jail, or Chris could have responded in kind, and then where would he be? How would those very real possible consequences of today have affected Will and his wife Jada? Common sense tells me that neither Will nor his wife Jada would be okay with any of those possible consequences! Thanks again, Patricia, for joining in and being willing to voice an opinion others may not agree with.*

DNA... HARDWIRED...

One of the things we have come to agree on in this conversation is that we don't all see common sense in the same way, but hopefully with discussions like this, we can get a little closer...

April 1, 2022 (social media post): *So I have been doing some more thinking on the Will Smith, Chris Rock, and David Chappelle situations and how good or bad or better or worse applies in both cases. Let's first try and determine what we are talking about when we say good or bad or better or worse. When we are talking about good or bad, we can be talking about whether something is good or bad from an ethical or moral point of view or good or bad from an intellectual decision-making point of view. I know there are other times we can use good or bad like in the case of whether or not the food tastes good or bad, was the movie good or bad, etc., but in this case, we are talking about good or bad from an ethical or moral point of view. Can we agree on that? I think Chris tried and is still trying to use the terms good or bad in both contexts when it suits his point at the time. I think we can now look at his decision based on whether it was the better or worse decision based on the financial aspect of the decision. You decide based on the fact it had been eighteen years or so since he made the decision to turn down the fifty million and he is now doing the very thing he would have been doing for those eighteen years, was it a better or worse decision? We can now also look at whether it was a good or bad decision from an intellectual decision-making point of view. I am not a math whiz, but I would imagine that if he continued doing what he stopped doing for those eighteen years or so, at approximately fifty million, every two years or so doing those eighteen years, considering inflation, he would probably be a lot better off financially! Some may ask, well, what about his good or bad decision from an ethical or moral standpoint? Again, he is still doing what he was doing when he turned down the fifty million all those years ago, and to me, he still seems like he is still not self-actualized!*

What about how good or bad or better or worse applies in the Will Smith and Chris Rock case? I think this one is easier to figure out! Will Smith either made a good or bad decision or a better or worse decision based on an intellectual basis! Just like with David Chappelle, we can speculate now, but time will be the true determinate factor! I know many will say hindsight is 20-20 and I agree, but that is why it is very important to try and use common sense and take as much into account as possible at the time you are making a decision while still realizing we are human...

April 4, 2022 (social media post): *Since there was so much interest and discussion on the topic of Will Smith and Chris Rock and how common sense did or did not play a role in the situation, I will be making a weekly post for discussion on common sense. As I have stated previously, I am writing a book on common sense, so much of the discussions will be on many of the subjects covered in the book. The posts and discussions will start on Mondays and last the week. It will be simply called*

"Weekly Common Sense Discussions!" Please be respectful of each other! We all have our thoughts and opinions, and we have a right to those thoughts and opinions!

April 4–April 10, 2022 (social medial post): *Let's first establish the fact that there IS a concept or theory called common sense! I have had some people tell me that there is no such thing as common sense! Well-known reputable sources such as* Merriam-Webster, Britannica, *and* Cambridge Dictionary *list common sense as a term and define it. Common sense would tell me that if they and other sources list it as existing, then it exists! For those that would still doubt those facts, then I am sure you will gain much from these discussions! Out of all the definitions I have come across, I prefer the following one: "Common sense, the knowledge that should be common to most people except babies and the mentally challenged!" So for this week's discussion, let's talk about your thoughts in general about common sense and why ALL people other than babies and the mentally challenged can't seem to grasp the concept?*

Response: AT: *I'm intrigued! Are you asking why we can't all agree on a definition of common sense? Or are you asking if "it" is common sense why can't we all agree on "it" (whatever it is)?*

My response: *Hello, AT! Hope all is well with you and the family! Good question! I think the dictionaries have given us a choice of definitions for common sense, and we should be free to choose which one or ones make sense to us.*

I totally get that we aren't all going to agree on which definition suits us, but just the idea that there are some of us, who aren't babies or are mentally challenged, who don't even believe that common sense exists requires discussion! The second part of your question, yes, if there is something that is at issue and fits one or more of the definitions of common sense defined in the dictionaries, why can't ALL of us, other than babies and the mentally challenged, agree on the issue and the resolution for resolving it? Prior to the start of writing my book on common sense, I didn't understand why that was so, but now that I have almost completed the book, things are so much clearer on the subject of common sense for me now! It makes it so much easier for me now to understand why we ALL at one time or another do or say things that just don't seem to make much sense to others! I am hoping by the end of our discussions, we will all be a little clearer on the subject.

Response: AT: *I was waiting to get home so I could respond using my laptop. I believe in common sense, but I think the reason we don't agree is because the definition has evolved (probably incorrectly). In other words, I don't think we use the phrase correctly much of the time. Based on the definition you gave (which I like), an example of common sense is...one minute I'm standing up but then I duck behind a couch... I didn't disappear just because you can't see me. We all know that (or should) but a baby doesn't. The baby hasn't learned the commonsense knowledge of object permanence yet. I think the problem/disagreement comes in because some people define common sense using a definition that includes legality or morality or other such concepts. Once we do that, we will never be able to agree on a definition for common sense or if a person is demonstrating common sense. So yes, I agree and believe in common sense (if I let go of a ball, it will fall to the ground because of gravity), but I don't think a situation like what occurred at the Oscars is a question of common sense. You could look at it with legal lenses, or moral lenses, or you could blame society, or maybe Mercury was in retrograde... One's opinion is going to be influenced on which lenses they are looking through (among other things)... but I don't think common sense applies in this situation because there is no "knowledge" that everyone should know.*

My response: *Thank you for your thoughtful and in-depth response! I agree with everything you said except that there was no common knowledge that* MOST *people other than babies and the mentally challenged should know. Shouldn't most people, other than babies and the mentally challenged, know that physically assaulting someone on worldwide TV was wrong and could have had drastic consequences like the person striking them back, the person suing them for a lot of money, a career-ending event, etc.? I already know that there are those that say that no, most people shouldn't know that! I will acknowledge that I am the one who is having a problem understanding this, and that is why I am doing this research and writing this book.*

My response: *Oh, I forgot to add, he could have gone to jail...*

Response: AT: *I am totally with you! In my world, that's the way it "should" be. Our laws and rules (man's and God's) are why many of us do and don't do things. It keeps order to our society. Luckily, I think most people do live by those rules for the most part. But for some people, there's a sense of entitlement or invincibility; maybe they are just in denial that anything bad will happen, or they just don't care (the words psychopath, sociopath, and narcissist are swimming in my mind right now). I think we clearly saw that the very reasons many of us don't assault people (the consequences) didn't happen in this case. So maybe we're the weird ones for thinking there would have and should have been consequences (no, I don't really believe that).*

My response: *Again, Thank you, AT! I agree with what you said, and you are helping me try and figure out why more of us don't use good judgment in our life decisions and choices!*

Response: BO (GO): *To me, it sounds like you are discussing both conscience and having good sense. One we have or most have from birth and the other taught or modeled for us by parents or other authority figures in our lives. Each of us are uniquely different by birth and experience, so the definitions are different for each of us. What makes sense to one may not to another.*

My response: *Hello, B! Hope all is well with you and G! You make some good points! Yes, we are discussing our ideas on what common sense is and our thoughts on common sense! Please* clarify, which are you saying we are born with, and which are we taught? I agree that our definitions of common sense may be different and what makes sense to one person may not make sense to another.

Response: BO (GO): *Born with a conscience—you learn common or good sense based on your environment, upbringing.*

My response: *Sounds good! Thanks!*

Response: JW: *Hey! Cousin! I feel that there is a chemical imbalance going on. When a person can't reason with what is going on or what is taking place…that is when common sense should kick in…but it doesn't because of whatever is screwed up in their head! Stress and daily lifestyle can trigger this shortcoming. Just my thoughts.*

My response: *Hello, Cousin! You are right! I am learning in writing this book that there are so many things that can affect the way we think and act! Many people around us think it is something as simple as poor reasoning, judgment, or we are just bad people, but in many cases, it can be beyond our control. I am not trying to make excuses for people, but if it does appear someone around us is having constant "living problems," then I would suggest and encourage professional intervention…*

April 5, 2022 (social medial post): *So the attachment is an example of what I would think MOST people, other than babies and the mentally challenged, would at least see as inappropriate for public wear and lacking a degree of common sense! I was just in Albertsons, the grocery store, and this lady in front of me was proudly wearing that shirt. She appeared to be at least fifty-five–sixty years of age. I suspect she may have had a particular audience in mind, but there were people with kids in the store. The lady directly in front of her had an eight- or nine-year-old little girl with her. Was the message for the little girl also? For those who would like to remind me of our right to freedom of speech, I get it. Hopefully, most of us, other than babies and the mentally challenged, would agree that certain speech should be reserved for certain situations, and making that statement in public was at least inappropriate… Thoughts?*

Response: AT: *Hahaha… I would say her decision makes no sense to me. Or I might say I think she made a poor choice in picking out her outside clothes. And I would say it was an inap-*

DNA... HARDWIRED...

propriate decision. I would also make a judgement and say her poor choice reflects her moral character (or lack of) and lack of consideration of those around her. But I'm not sure, I think common sense is a factor. Did you notice the other T-shirt: Good luck. 😀

My response: *Yes, I did see the other shirt! I believe there are more of us, people with positive attitudes and wish people well, than them, people who are negative and don't wish others well...*

Response: CDFJ: *In all situations, that is a lack of morals and character.*

My response: *Hello, Cousin! Hope all is well with you, HJ, and the family! Thank you for joining in! Very good point!*

Response: FD: *Absolutely. It's as if we have lost our sense of propriety in this era. It makes me oh so sad.*

Response: DB: *Wow, that's crazy.*

My response: *Hello, Cousin DB! Hope all is well with you and the family! Thank you for the input! Yes, it is crazy, but I am sure you have seen things just as crazy! I am just happy that we are having these discussions and hopefully can reach some of these people that are doing crazy things and hopefully affect their attitudes and behaviors in a positive way!!*

Response: DB: *Hello, cousin. I hope and pray so too.*

My response: *Hello, FD, hope you and your husband are enjoying your travels! Thank you for your input! I think these people have been with us for a long time. We are now in a time where they are more emboldened to show and express themselves! As I said, this lady looks like she is*

25

fifty-five–sixty years. I don't think she got that way in the last few years...

Response: FD: *I'm saddened by that sort of behavior. It makes me a bit ashamed of us as a society and as a generation.*

Response: LC: *I agree with u 100 percent, Mr. James, some people don't have any common sense.* 😠😠😠

My response: *Hello, LC, thanks for joining in on the conversation!*

Response: PW: *Oh wow!*

Response: AS: *When people wear things like that, it's just a reflection of who they are! Sad. It says a lot about their character!*

My response: *Hey, AS! Yes, I am just trying to figure out why so many people who are so smart and normal in most day-to-day situations sometimes find themselves doing something like that! Chances are she is just a regular person with a regular family living a regular life but has blind spots at times like most of us!*

Response: AS: *No, I disagree. I think that's how she lives her life! Like I said, it shows her character! You've got to be pretty bold to wear a shirt like that. I'm just saying.*

My response: *I won't disagree... I am just hoping you are wrong...*

Response: AS.: *Me too but doubtful in the world we live in today! No human compassion...or common sense!*

Response: LC: *Excellent example of common sense...or lack of. Yes, I absolutely believe in freedom of speech. However, common sense asks just because I can, should I? This person is, yes, probably directing her voice at a specific audience without care to whomever else sees* it. *Prime example of lack of compassion and common sense.*

My response: *Hello, LC! Hope all is well with you, FC, and the kids! Thanks for joining in on the conversation! I agree with your comments! I think most people would agree with most of the comments and opinions so far in the discussion! This really gives me hope and reassures me that most of us are good people and have good intentions!*

Response: RD: *Totally inappropriate.*

Response: RC: *I agree, she didn't just get this way in the last few years, but now she feels comfortable enough to express it openly without fearing any consequences. As a society, we will NEVER be able to "change what we tolerate." Sad.*

My response: *Hey, RC! I totally agree! I watched her in the store for about fifteen to twenty minutes, and it was almost like she was daring anyone to approach her about the shirt! I agree with the tolerate part. I had an opportunity to approach her in a respectful nonthreatening manner, but truthfully, I was afraid of the reaction I felt I was going to receive from her! Thank you for reminding me that I have a responsibility to do the right thing even when it may be uncomfortable!*

Response: FR Sr.: *What would make you buy a shirt with that on it?*

My response: *Hey, FR, Sr.! Hope all is well with you and the family! I am really going to have to get with you on one of my trips back to Pittsburgh! The reason someone would do that is the reason we are having these discussions and why I am writing a book on common sense. If you have been following the discussions, many people are providing some good insight into why some of us might decide to purchase a shirt like that and wear it in public. I am sure we will never be able to get into other people's minds, but hopefully, these discussions will help us get a better understanding of them and ourselves.*

Response: GO: *While I am also dismayed at the choices this woman made, the f-word has become acceptable speech to a large segment of society. The sentiment expressed on the shirt is also accepted by many people. And if you ask the woman if she or her sympathizers have "common sense," what do you suppose her response would be? We have devolved to the point that the rights of a single individual are more important than the rights of society.*

My response: *GO, I agree with all that you said, including the part about how she and her sympathizers would probably view her actions as sensible! My hope is that there are a lot more of us than there are of them, and we can eventually turn this thing around! Hopefully the statement RC made, "As a society, we will NEVER be able to 'change what we tolerate,'" will become a battle cry for this change!*

Response: GO: *Had our children been taught respect for their elders, tolerance for the opinions of others, attire appropriate to the situation, civil discourse, etc., then perhaps we could return to a kinder, gentler nation. But by words and actions, adults taught their children it is okay to be crude, vulgar, intolerant, and indifferent to the feelings of others. I believe the United States is racing to become a nation of haves and have-nots. Those who*

DNA... HARDWIRED...

have marketable skills and are able to interact with others will succeed. The rest will not.

My response: *GO, I am just seeing this post... Yes, I completely agree with you, especially the part about the parent's role in all of this! Again, I don't know this lady, but she may have kids, possibly grandkids, what message is she sending to them? I know there were many kids in the store, and I suspect many of them saw her shirt and its message. Imagine all of the possible messages and signals this adult parent and grandparent figure sent to them?*

Response: RH: *Personally, absolutely disgusting! Nothing to do with common sense, however, more of a lack of decency and respect for others as well of herself...typical of these times. It's appalling but not surprising in the least... 🙏 God help us!*

My response: *Hello, Cousin! Hope all is well with you and JH! Yes, you make some good points*

Response: JG: *Perfectly said!*

Response: JG: *Error in comment. Hit wrong icon. People have lost respect for others and themselves. Said day*

My response: *Hey, Cousin! Hope all is well! I agree that lack of respect is also an issue...*

Response: AC: *I love the shirt. I bought all the kids small sizes for Christmas.*

My response: *Hello, AC, I know you and I am sure you did NOT do that because your wife would kill you! For those of you that don't know AC, believe me, he is kidding...*

Response: NS.: *Disgusting and so inappropriate.*

Response: RJ: *A person wearing that kind of shirt is being provocative. She's trying to convey a message and probably is half hoping to elicit* feedback. It's a strong wardrobe choice. Kind of like going to Tucson decked in a Sun Devils shirt but more profane.

My response: *Hey, RJ! Miss you at the gym! I agree with your thoughts about her wanting to convey a message and was hoping for feedback. I also suspect she was looking for a confrontation from someone…anyone! I am just puzzled as to why she subjected every stranger she ran into to her profanity and why she sought confrontation from those same strangers? RJ, I know we will never understand why many people do some of the things they do, but I am trying to get a better understanding… Thanks for your input, RJ.*

Response: RJ: *What's unfortunate (for her mostly) is that your only takeaway from having encountered her will be her shirt. Presumably she has some good qualities. Probably a family. People she loves. Thoughts that touch on higher and better things than her shirt would lead you to believe. But you'll never know those things because her shirt scared you off.*

My response: *I agree with all the things you said about her probably being a "normal" person with some good qualities and a family. I do believe that people who wear clothing with messages written on that clothing for all to see can and often do tell us a lot about who they are and their beliefs. For example, if you didn't know me and I was wearing a shirt that said I hate all White people, would you believe what I had written on my shirt or come to some other conclusion?*

Response: ELR III: *Not that it matters, but what did it say on the front?*

DNA... HARDWIRED...

My response: *There was some sort of small logo up around the shoulder area. It looked like two crossed rifles with some wording I couldn't make out...*

Response: MM: *My sentiments exactly, that's ridiculous immature and ignorant. Wow!*

Response: AWG: *Totally agree... We should have sent for that little disgusting boy that urinates on everything and person... By the way, yet another inappropriate message and illustration. I guess that leaves us some comfort... The message DID NOT bless us with illustration.*

April 11–17, 2022 (social medial post): *Okay, we made it through our first Weekly Common Sense Discussion! Thank you! I greatly appreciate all your input and support! Our goal was to determine or establish the fact that there is or is not such a thing called common sense! I think we did determine that common sense does exist! Some of us would prefer to call it by other names such as sense, ethics, morality, sound judgment, choices, etc., but I think most of us agree that there is knowledge that most people, other than babies and the mentally challenged, should know! For simplicity and to humor me, let's call it common sense. So for this week, I would like for us to discuss two other keywords or terms you will see throughout our discussions that will hopefully help us better understand common sense and the roles these words or terms play in common sense!*

First is DNA, the carrier of genetic information. Let's look at this as primarily the "physical" part of our makeup that helps make us who we are physically, i.e., eye color, hair color, height, skin color, etc. Not much we can do about changing that part of our makeup as a living being other than some medical procedure possibly, and that only changes the physical appearance, not the actual DNA structure itself.

Second "hardwired," genetically or innately determined, pertaining to or being a deep-rooted and relatively unmodifiable behavior or thought pattern in most cases! I like to think of this as our "psychological, mental, or emotional" part of our makeup or being that helps make us who we are from an attitudinal, thought, and behavior place. I strongly suspect this is why we as human beings have a problem with common sense most of the time. Through my research, I have not been able to find or see any other possible reason, other than for babies and those with mental challenges, for our complete lack of intelligence or common sense in many instances!

For example, if I asked you what your favorite and least favorite colors were, could you tell me? I suspect you could. If I offered you $1,000,000 to change your most favorite color to your least favorite color and your least favorite color to your most favorite color, could you immediately do so on demand? I don't mean could you tell me you did it, but could you immediately intellectualize and mentally internally change how you truly felt about the colors simply based upon a request in exchange for a large sum of money? I suspect you could not. If we can't consciously change our thoughts or behavior on something as simple and unimportant as our most favorite or least favorite *colors on request or demand for a large sum of money, how can we change other more difficult and impactful aspects of our thoughts or life like race, religion, or politics for free? This is an example of being hardwired.*

What are your thoughts on these two terms and their possible relationship to common sense?

Response: RC: *Wow, I never looked at it from that perspective. When you put it in those terms, I would have to say that maybe we just have to lofty expectations in human behavior. Unfortunately, I agree with you, we shouldn't expect an individual's opinions and behaviors to deviate from their core beliefs! I'm not saying that people can't and won't change, but we are talking about the majority in this situation.*

My response: *RC! Thank you! You have just illustrated a key factor in common sense! If there is something we may not be aware of or understand, which happens to all of us at one time or another, but is explained to us, most of us should get it! The problem is that there are some of us that just won't get it no matter how it is explained to us! There are many possible reasons for this, and hopefully, we will discuss the reasons at some point in our discussions. As far as our expectations of human behavior, I think that most of us do get it! Especially after it is pointed out and explained to us! One of the problems is that the minority, who at times don't get it, have the loudest voices and in many cases drown out the voices of common sense! I agree with statements on core beliefs.*

April 18–24, 2022 (social medial post): *This week's discussion will continue to focus on some key points and establishing a foundation for our discussions on common sense. We will cover the following in more detail in later discussions, but nowhere in any of the definitions or descriptions of common sense did I find any mention of God, race, religion, beliefs, gender, politics, etc., or any other thoughts that wasn't based in fact, logic, or just plain common sense! So that we are clear, God, race, religion, beliefs, gender, politics, etc. all play a role in my day-to-day life, so I am NOT suggesting that those things shouldn't be important or play a role in your day-to-day life! Race, politics, and religion are probably three of the biggest and most common violators of commonsense rules or principles! Yet those are the three topics many people are frequently heard saying, "If you don't want to lose or ruin good relationships, do not discuss race, politics, or religion!" The three topics that probably have the most impact on our daily lives and many feel and believe we should not discuss them! This is just one of many instances that just doesn't seem to make very much common sense to me! My question to you is, from a practical and day-to-day place, are you focusing enough day-to-day on other things in your life like you personally, love, happiness, kindness, peace, purpose, time, health, facts, science, logic, etc.... Thoughts?*

P.S. Please feel free to post and comment on anything that may or may not relate to the specific topic of discussion for the week.

DNA... HARDWIRED...

April 25–May 1, 2022 (social medial post): *Weekly Common Sense discussion: Now that we have focused on some key points and established a foundation for our discussions on common sense, let's discuss some real and practical ways common sense affects us in our day-to-day lives! Going forward, I will make every attempt to not voice my personal opinions in our discussions! My goal is to get as much discussion and cross flow of information so that we can all learn and benefit from what everyone has to share! If you truly want to know my personal opinion on a topic, please private message me! The topic for this week is COVID-19! I know that this is a "hot button" topic, and everyone has their own personal opinion and has a right to that personal opinion, but I think it is an excellent and important real-life topic to discuss when trying to figure out and understand why there is such disagreement and controversy on the subject! Please remember that we will be respectful of everyone's thoughts and opinions in our discussions!*

PLEASE SHARE OUR DISCUSSIONS TO YOUR FAMILY AND FRIENDS' FACEBOOK PAGES SO THAT THEY MAY PARTICIPATE AND BENEFIT FROM OUR DISCUSSIONS ALSO! THANK YOU!

Response: AT: *Why is there such disagreement and controversy on the subject of COVID? I think there's a lot of disagreement on everything. I think that is normal and expected. The more people there are, the more opinions we'll have. What confuses me is why there is so much anger over disagreeing. I don't know why COVID (and everything else) has become so politicized. Why can't people be pro-mask or anti-vaccine or anything else without it being tied to a political party? You know what else I think...remember the days of 5:00 p.m. and 10:00 p.m. news. The news programs were only thirty minutes long. The first fifteen minutes was news, then weather, sports, and any community/feel-good story. They had fifteen minutes to give you the highlights of any local to world events. If you wanted more details, you read the paper. But if you wanted an opinion, you read the opinion column. You had to seek out the opinion of others. Now the news channels go all day long, and they are mainly opinions with very little of "just the facts." So people are inundated with opinions and assuming those opinions are news. They are just opinions! Seek out the facts, make your own opinion, and stop being mad just because someone thinks differently than you do. In addition, thinking differently from time to time from the political party you align yourself with is not a betrayal. It just means you have your own opinions...which were formed because of your own unique experiences (which we talked about a few weeks ago).*

My response: *AT, thank you! You made some points better than I ever could! Hopefully, as we get more into these discussions and people feel more comfortable sharing their views and opinions, we will be able to get a better understanding of why we can't agree to disagree without so much anger and division! I agree that politics and the media play such a huge role in our lives today that it is very hard to get agreement on much if it is outside of our own political parties' views or whatever*

DNA... HARDWIRED...

direction the media wants to take us that day! I personally love politics and the media, but I agree with you, gather as much FACTUAL information as possible and come to your OWN conclusions on a subject! I think I have a solution to that problem, and I will share it with the group at a later time when we get into the discussion on politics! Thanks again, Angela, and I encourage others to get involved in the discussions and make their voices heard! This is how we grow and learn together.

May 9–15, 2022 (social medial post): *If your answer to the question of whether or not common sense is a choice was no, it is not a choice, then for you, the discussion may be over! You may have decided you have no control over your thoughts and behavior! If your answer is yes, common sense is a choice, then let's continue the discussion! Your yes answer creates more questions like how much control do we have over commonsense choices? Can we learn how to make better commonsense choices? Yes and yes! What are some ways to learn how to make better commonsense choices? One way to learn how to make better commonsense choices is to practice using common sense by being more aware and reflecting on situations before you make decisions:*

- *Compare the risks and rewards of a decision before choosing what to do.*
- *Don't do things that you KNOW are bad for you or others.*
- *Trust your initial feelings so you don't overanalyze a situation.*

- *Look at the situation from other perspectives and think it through clearly.*
- *Ask someone you trust, who has a proven history of exhibiting sound judgment, if you aren't sure about your decision.*
- *Think before you speak or act.*
- *Understand that it's okay to make a wrong decision occasionally.*

As you practice, you will develop more common sense, and you will be able to make smarter choices and decisions!

COMMON SENSE ORIGINS

So where does the concept of common sense originate from? Are we born with it, or are we taught common sense? I suspect it is a little of both! For example, since birth, if we encounter something fearful to us for the first time, let's just say a very large and mean-looking barking dog threatening to attack us, in all probability we would try and run away and avoid it at all costs because common sense would tell us that it would probably harm us if we let it get too close to us! In that case, that is something we probably wouldn't need to be taught but would learn very quickly on our own! Some refer to this as the "fight or flight" response. Learning to cross the street safely growing up is probably one of those occasions where we will probably need to be taught that piece of common sense and early on! That is one of those occasions where we probably shouldn't rely on someone to learn on their own in their own good time! Are there things in life we seem to never learn to approach with a degree of common sense? Yes, that is what prompted me to write this book! For example, most of us have been taught that we should treat people the way we want to be treated, but there seems to be many people who either were never taught or never learned on their own this very simple and important lesson in life or is just choosing to ignore it! Common sense would say that if you treat people badly, then they probably won't treat you nicely! If you continually lie to people, people probably won't trust or believe you after some time! There are many in "the other" group who are not babies or have mental challenges who don't appear to get or understand these and many other logical or common sense concepts!

We are all probably guilty of lacking a degree of common sense at one time or another in our lives. Are we ignorant and just not that bright? Probably in some cases, but I think lacking common sense many times is just part of being human! We are human and we all have blind spots. We are not perfect and aren't meant to be perfect!

What is the difference between logic and common sense? Many people think they are the same, but they are not. Logic is used to reach a conclusion using the most accurate and scientific route available to mankind. Common sense is not always accurate and can be based on one's biases, assumptions, social acceptance, and not always factual. Logical thinking is a process that should involve no emotions and be based on facts! Not so much so with common sense many times, especially with the "other" group.

Is common sense a choice, an act of selecting or making a decision when faced with two or more possibilities? Yes, I think it is a choice. But the question for me is how much actual control do we have in making that choice? I believe the "hardwired effect" has a lot more to do with many of our "free" choices or decisions than a logical thought process or common sense! This is a logical reason or explanation for many of our poor decisions or choices.

PERCEPTION OR BELIEF VERSUS REALITY

If common sense is defined as situations or facts that are shared by *nearly* all people except babies and those with mental challenges, then why aren't *all* situations or facts agreed upon by *all* people except babies and those with mental challenges? Could it be one's perception…a way of regarding, understanding, or interpreting something, a mental impression? Or could it be one's belief…trust, faith, or confidence in someone or something that causes the nearly all or the "other" group of people to not see common sense for what it is? Is one's perception or belief (an idealistic or hypothetical idea) the same as reality (the world or the state of things as they actually exist and are proven to be true)?

Perception or belief is not necessarily true reality or fact…but one's perception or belief can *become* a person's reality! Can you possibly see how this can be a definite barrier to common sense in many cases? There are many people who perceive or truly believe that the Black race is inferior to the White race. Is this a fact or reality or just their perception or belief? As a person who believes he possesses a healthy degree of common sense and logic, I would say that it is a person's perception or belief and *not* reality that the Black race is inferior to the White race or any other race! I would dare to say that *no* race is superior or inferior to any other race! I am a firm believer that, as stated in the Bible ("We are all equally made in God's image" [Genesis 1:26–28]) and proven through science, we are all created equally as human beings! There are some physical attributes of a race or socioeconomic factors that might *seem* to indicate some superiority of one group over another, but these are limited cases. For example, the Caucasian and Black races are generally taller than most of the Asian countries, so therefore, one might tend to believe that Caucasian and Black basketball players would be superior to Asians in the sport of basketball. But of course, we realize that there are tall Asians and short Caucasians and Blacks, so this isn't always the case that Caucasian and Black will always be superior to Asians in the sport of basketball.

There are still some people, even in the present year, who believe that the earth is flat and not round or spherical. They truly believe it is flat no matter what proof or facts you provide to them! Is this just their perceptions, or is this a fact that the earth is flat? Based on man's ability to travel and satellites and other technology outside the earth's atmosphere, it is a proven fact the earth is indeed round or spherical! So what do you do with those people who don't believe we have traveled or put satellites or other technology outside the earth's atmosphere? *Nothing!* Through my research, I couldn't find *any* solution to this cognitive dissonance and the backfire effect!

Just like whether or not the earth is flat, there are some people who believe that when the sun goes down and it gets dark, the sun is like a light bulb and is off during the time of darkness. Would their opinions change if they lived in Barrow, Alaska, where there's two months straight of darkness in the winter, from about November 18 to January 22? But in the summer, the sun doesn't completely set for about eighty-two days, from roughly May 11 until July 31? The examples of the flat earth or the sun being off at night are easily provable and consistently factual! What about a refrigerator light? Does it go out when the refrigerator door is closed? Many will automatically say yes because we have a basic understanding of how the refrigerator door mechanism that shuts the light off works. What if I told you not necessarily *every* time in *every* instance does the light go out! What if I explained to you that maybe there are occasions where the mechanism that shuts the light off upon the door closing malfunctioned? Would you be willing to consider and change your opinion and say that there may be rare occasions where the door mechanism failed, and the light didn't shut off? I suspect that most reasonable people who aren't babies or mentally challenged and have a healthy dose of common sense would agree with that premise. I would also suspect that there are those in the "other" group that would continue to insist the light always go out no matter what.

I suspect that most reasonable people who are provided with reasonable explanations and facts will see most common sense situations for what they are no matter what their perceptions or beliefs may have been prior. My confusion is with the "other" group, who even after being presented with reasonable explanations and provable facts still seem to not be able to grasp or understand the situation for what it truly is from a commonsense perspective!

Observation: The hunter and the hunted have different perceptions and opinions of hunting… The oppressor and the oppressed have a different perception and opinion of oppression! Which one's perception and opinion is reality? How would an unbiased outside observer see the situation? Can there truly be an unbiased observer? Even though we may not have, as they say, "a dog in the fight," it is hard for us not to have our personal thoughts or feelings one way or the other on a subject or situation. I would suspect that for the hunter, the hunted, the oppressor, and the oppressed, their perceptions are a reality for them. Can you see how this can further complicate the concept of common sense?

> May 16–22, 2022 (social medial post): *Based on last week's discussion, we agree common sense is a choice in most cases, and we have control over our thoughts and behaviors! We learned that we could learn how to make better commonsense choices by being more aware and practicing commonsense techniques!*
>
> *This week's topic of discussion is "What role, if any, does one's perceptions or beliefs play in how we apply common sense in a situation?" To add to the discussions, let's add real-life events, when possible, to see how they may or may not apply. Please remember that every-*

one has a right to their opinions, and we will remain respectful with our comments!

So the young man that shot the thirteen people in Buffalo, New York, this past Saturday, what role did his possible perceptions or beliefs play in his applying common sense in that situation?

Response: AT: *James, this is a tough one. I'm not sure what "common sense" is here. If you kill people, it's illegal, and you will go to jail. If you kill people, it's immoral, and you'll be judged by God. Killing people is wrong? Or maybe there's a belief that self-actualization is the goal. It's focusing on the bigger picture. The person who breaks into a lab and frees the mice from drug testing might say they are self-actualized and that doing the "right" thing is more important than doing the legal thing. Maybe the Buffalo guy was applying some twisted sense of self-actualization or purpose. Or maybe his perceptions (delusions) or beliefs are being driven by mental illness. Or maybe his heart is just full of hate and pain, and the only thing he can think of to do is it to make others hurt more than he's hurting. My bottom line is I don't know what made the Buffalo guy (or anyone else who does these kinds of things) do the things he did. I think it has A LOT to do with their beliefs and perceptions, but I'm not sure where common sense comes in to play or if it even does.*

My response: *AT, you and I agree that this is not an example of what most people would call an example of the application of common sense! Evidently, this individual, and too many more like him, think, feel, and believe that* what he was thinking and did made perfect sense to them! As far as his motive(s), I agree we don't truly know why he chose to do what he did, but let's just go with what he said and what his actions were leading up to the shooting... "Hatred toward Black people!" I think that this is one of the biggest problems we as a society and human race are faced with today..."HATRED!" Hate because of someone's skin color, race, national origin, religion, sexual orientation, economic status, age, etc.! You mentioned that his perceptions and beliefs probably had a lot to do with his decision to do what he did, and I agree! We will talk about one's perceptions and one's beliefs and their connection to common sense in later discussions, but for now, one's perception or belief is not necessarily true reality or fact, but one's perception or belief CAN become a person's reality as in the case of the Buffalo shooter...

Response: AT: *James, I totally agree. I think hatred is one of our biggest problems. I'm torn on whether it is getting worse or if some people are just getting more vocal about what they've always believed. With social media, we've certainly seen what appears to be a huge uptick of hatred from people hiding behind a keyboard. I've said this before, and I truly believe it. It's not what's in a person's hand, it's what's in a person's heart. If we want to end these senseless murders, we have to figure out how to take away the hate. I don't have the answer, and I'm not sure anyone else does either. And...I totally agree with you about perception and reality! I can't stand when people say perception is reality. Perception is their reality but not necessarily true or real world. John Hinckley believed Jodie Foster was talking to him via Taxi Driver, and if he killed the president, it would impress her. That was certainly his perception, but it was not real reality.*

My response: *AT, you are exemplifying knowledge that most people, other than babies and the mentally challenged, should possess, which we have agreed is called common sense, right? This is why I am so interested in researching and having these discussions on common sense! I am convinced that there are far more people who think and feel the way that you and I do, but they remain quiet! The others have become more vocal as you stated! I think part of the answer is for others to get involved more and not just when there is an incident! We need to speak out at any time we see or hear our relatives, friends, and neighbors speak of hate!*

Observation: *The hunter and the hunted have different perceptions and opinions of hunting... The oppressor and the oppressed have different perceptions and opinions of oppression! Which one's perception and opinion is reality? How would an impartial outside observer see the situation? Can there truly be an impartial observer? Even though we may not have, as they say, "a dog in the fight," it is hard for us not to have our personal thoughts or feelings one way or another on a subject or situation. I would suspect that for the hunter, the hunted, the oppressor, and the oppressed, their perceptions are a reality for them. Can you see how this can further complicate the concept of common sense? I suspect that most reasonable peo-*

ple who are provided with reasonable explanations and facts will see most commonsense situations for what they are no matter what their perceptions or beliefs may have been prior. My confusion is with the "other" group, who even after being presented with reasonable explanations and facts still seem to not be able or refuse to grasp or understand the situation for what it truly is from a commonsense perspective!

Response: SW: *I think we are all biased. Proof of this is with identical twins. Nature versus nurture. While two people can have the same DNA at birth, they still live very different lives from each other. I'm a scientist at heart and by trade, so statistically I do think there is common sense, and it would fall into the bell curve analogy. Where the majority, depending on your statistical models, sometimes greater and less majorities have opinions about common sense. There will always be outliers on the fringe having a differing opinion. I think it's fair to say most people agree murder is wrong, but clearly there is a fringe minority that disagrees because they do it. Not all topics are that cut and dry. However, common sense also can't be defined unless we share common language. The next question I'd ask you is to define oppressor and oppressed, hunter and hunted. I'm a hunter of deer, fish, ducks, etc., what is the perception of the animal I'm hunting? I don't think we know because we can't apply human thought to animals. Death to an animal (nonhuman) has very different means, I would suspect. Same with oppressor and oppressed. Would Biden be considered an oppressor for vaccine mandates or Trump an oppressor for a strong stance on the border? To me that's where the bell curve comes in and the question has to be clearly defined. I'm sure I rambled and didn't answer your question at all, but I really enjoy reading your questions and pondering them. I think answers to some of these questions are a key to bringing our country back together.*

My response: *SS, thank you for your comments! All very enlightening, well thought out, and presented! I didn't think you rambled at all, and you answered questions and definitely gave us some more things to think about! A couple of thoughts on some of your responses. On the comment about common sense can't be defined unless we share a common language. Does that apply in all instances of the application of common sense or maybe in certain instances or situations? I only know one language, but I would suspect that if I attacked anyone speaking another language, they would probably try to defend themselves. Some may call that by another name like survival, fight or flight, or something else, but for me, it's just common sense not to attack anyone without the possibility of some form of retaliation! I don't know a lot about other cultures, but I suspect that there are some things that are universal across the human race like the desire for survival...no matter the language you may speak! I am sure there may be some cultures that do not believe in defending themselves or their loved ones, but I would suspect that there aren't many cultures like that. Remember our definition of common sense, "knowledge that most people, except babies and the mentally challenged, should know!" The definition isn't limited to a specific language or culture. Your question about defining oppressor and oppressed, hunter and hunted. I agree that we don't know what an animal, other than the human animal, may think about oppressor and oppressed or hunter and hunted, but here are my thoughts on it. I was using it as an analogy, but we do know what those terms mean. I am only guessing, but I would suspect that the things that you hunt have some sort of instinct that tells them that you do not mean them well, and that is why they try to avoid having contact with you! Again, we can put whatever label we choose on that instinct, but most animals that humans have had contact with, especially negative contact, have a sense, some call it instinct, of what might result from that contact. Many of us have or have had domestic pets, so we have personally observed how much sense, or lack thereof, they may have. Maybe a better example of the hunter and the hunted would be the authorities hunting a criminal! I am sure they will have different perceptions of the hunt! On your point about oppression, I love the way you used both Pres. Biden and Pres. Trump equally in your analogy! I think we need more of that! It will help bring our country back together as you stated! I know the two examples of possible oppression you used were just that, an example of possible oppression! Oppression is defined as an "unjust or cruel exercise of authority or power!" This is an example of where one's perception or belief may come into play. I per-*

sonally don't see either of the actions by the two presidents as unjust or cruel! I totally get your point and your thoughts though! There are many on either side who do believe their actions were unjust or cruel! Maybe a clearer example of oppressor and oppressed might be women viewed as property in some cultures! More of us need to get to the point where we don't all necessarily agree but are willing to consider other points of view! Thanks again, SS!

Response: SS: *James, thanks for the response, without going into novels, because Facebook isn't a great venue for long-answer formats. The only clarification I wanted to make was about language. One challenge as humans is there are many "languages," but our society is even having a hard time using the same language of English to define terms. There's a push for an evolution of words to have different meanings, which makes communication difficult even for people that speak the same language (English, etc.). If we can't even agree on common definitions in one language, how can we communicate to people of other languages or even try to interpret history? My point more or less is that the more agreement in language, the more we can define cultural norms and maybe common sense. One point I heard from Yeon mi Park that was surprising is that North Korea doesn't have a word for love because they want to control their population by only allowing any feeling of love, admiration, etc. as for their supreme leader. When she came to the US and even South Korea, she experienced such a different world that she didn't know existed. That's an extreme example but shows language being controlled and changed to bias a population and control common sense. Anyway, there I go again! It's been fun talking/typing!*

My response: *Thank you, SS! This is why I want to have these discussions! There is so much knowledge and insight out there that we can all benefit from if we are just willing to communicate and share! Thank you for sharing and increasing my knowledge and awareness!*

Response: AT: *I agree with everything you said. I think our perceptions and beliefs do help us form our opinions, even when we don't have dog in the fight, even when it doesn't involve us in any way. I also agree that reasonable people can "see commonsense situations for what they are." You're confused by the "others." A very wise man once told me that I wouldn't expect a person in a wheelchair to just get up and walk and then get mad at him or her when they don't. There's going to be a small percentage of the population that just isn't going to think and act like the majority...for all sorts of reasons. You and I know this all too well.*

My response: *The wheelchair analogy is very good; I like it! I agree that not all of us are going to think and act alike, and that shouldn't be our expectation. I just hope more of us will be able to think more alike and come together on many of the major issues facing the world like world peace, world hunger, homelessness, all types of abuse, hate, and division, etc.... Hopefully, it can start with these kinds of discussions on a more local level...*

Response: AT: *The wheelchair analogy came from you. You were my wise friend. You were helping me to manage my expectations.*

My response: *How funny. Lol! I am happy it stuck with you so you could remind me…*

Response: AS: *Common sense is not in everyone's DNA; they don't teach it in school or give you a college degree for it. You either have it or you don't! Therefore, everyone will see situations differently… I often find myself getting frustrated when people don't see things the same way as I do then I have to say to myself, "Stop expecting them to understand or see it your way, we are all different." I think that's where communication comes in, and we need to talk things out.*

My response: *I agree! I think being aware of what you said will go a long way in helping us have a better understanding of why we may think differently and therefore have a better understanding of each other…*

INTELLIGENCE

For this guide, intelligence is described as the ability to learn or understand or to deal with new and/or difficult situations. The following are some factors that affect the ability to learn:

- *Meaningfulness Effect*: The more meaningful the subject is to us, the easier it is for us to remember. If the content doesn't make sense or isn't relevant enough, learners will have a harder time learning.
- *Practice Effect:* Practice or rehearsal enhances retention.
- *Interference Effect:* It happens when a learner tries to remember old materials previously learned while learning new material. An interference effect is usually always negative.
- *Transfer Effect:* Takes place when prior learning or old material makes learning new content easier.
- *Text-Organization Effect:* Break up text so information is easier to read

How does intelligence relate to common sense? Intelligence is knowledge about something, and common sense is knowing how to use that knowledge practically at the proper place and time. Intelligence and common sense are not synonyms; they are not interchangeable. Many have a very high IQ or intelligence level but lack common sense and vice versa; many have a very high degree of common sense but are lacking in high IQ. Intelligence is a complex trait that is influenced by both genetic and environmental factors. Is intelligence inheritable? It has been determined that a degree of intelligence is indeed inherited!

May 28, 2022 (social medial post): Intelligence is knowledge about something, and common sense is knowing how to use that knowledge practically at the proper place and time. Intelligence and common sense are not synonyms; they are not interchangeable. Many have a very high IQ or intelligence level but lack common sense and vice versa; many have a very high degree of common sense but are lacking in high IQ. Intelligence is a complex trait influenced by genetic and environmental factors. Is intelligence inheritable? It has been determined that a degree of intelligence is indeed inherited!

Ignorance is described as a lack of knowledge, education, or awareness. What role does ignorance play in common sense? Mark Twain was known to have said that we are all ignorant to varying degrees of different things. No one knows all. An ignorant person may lack intelligence and common sense. Is ignorance a choice? At first thought, common sense would say no. If not a choice, then what is it? Is it in our DNA? Is it a case of being hardwired? There have been studies that indicate that many times we choose to remain ignorant of the truth or facts because we are afraid of the potential pain or unpleasantness associated with knowing the truth! This avoidance of truth or facts, or deliberate ignorance, affects our behavior many times, thereby making us appear to lack intelligence or common sense. It has been said that "it ain't so much people's ignorance that does harm as they're knowing so darned much that ain't so" (Josh Billings).

DNA... HARDWIRED...

Response: FG: *Oh, how I loved this* 💜💜💜
My response: *Thank you, FG! Hope all is well with you guys!*

IGNORANCE

For this guide, ignorance is described as a lack of knowledge, education, or awareness. What role does ignorance play in common sense? Mark Twain was known to have said that we are all ignorant to varying degrees of different things. No one knows all. An ignorant person may lack intelligence and common sense. Is ignorance a choice? At first thought, common sense would say no. If not a choice, then what is it? Is it in our DNA? Is it a case of being hardwired? There have been studies that indicate that many times we choose to remain ignorant to the truth or facts because we are afraid of the potential pain or unpleasantness associated with knowing the truth!

Observation: As of January 2022, almost two-third of Republicans believed that Pres. Joe Biden did not legitimately win the 2020 election and only 60 percent of Americans overall believed he won fairly. Approximately 30 percent Republicans say they will never accept Biden as president. The belief in widespread fraud among Republicans persists in spite of many probes and court rulings that found no evidence of fraud or any other interference that affected the election results! The belief of fraud was so strong among many Republicans that thousands attacked the Capitol on January 6, 2021, in order to stop the election results from being certified!

This avoidance of truth or facts, or deliberate ignorance, affects our behavior many times, thereby making us appear to lack intelligence or common sense.

> Nothing in all the world is more dangerous than sincere ignorance and conscientious stupidity.
>
> - Martin Luther King Jr

Observation: It has been said that "it ain't so much people's ignorance that does the harm as their knowing so darned much that ain't so" (*Josh Billings*).

MENTAL ILLNESS/MENTAL HEALTH DISORDERS

Mental illness, also called mental health disorders, refers to a wide range of mental health conditions or disorders that affect your mood, thinking and behavior. Examples of mental disorders include depression, anxiety disorders, schizophrenia, eating disorders and addictive behaviors. Many people have mental health concerns from time to time. This is why it will be very difficult to determine if a person's apparent lack of common sense is actually a lack of common sense or a mental disorder. A mental health concern becomes a mental disorder when ongoing signs and symptoms cause frequent stress and affect one's ability to function. It is usually at this point the mental disorder is diagnosed and it becomes easier to determine if an individual's behavior or attitude is a result of a lack of common sense or a mental disorder.

If you find that you or someone close to you frequently exhibit what appears to be a lack of common sense routinely, I would encourage a counselor or therapist be consulted to see if there is reason for concern. Whether it is a case of true lack of common sense or a case of mental illness, the situation should be addressed by a professional since both conditions are serious.

> May 30–June 5, 2022 (social medial post): *This week's topic of discussion is "What role, if any, does mental illness or mental health disorders play in common sense?" I have stated previously, I like to try and tie what is going on in our daily lives with some of the topics we*

discuss. So your thoughts on the school shooting in Texas and how mental illness might play a role...

Response: MM: *I won't say much right now except our nation seems to make excuses for some people when it comes to common sense and using mental health as a crutch it seems, as we watch how things were handled even with the shooter in Texas or Buffalo or in most of the over three hundred incidents we've had.*

Honestly exhausting because not everyone gets the opportunity to even obtain mental health resources to address the root. But when someone just blatantly makes a plan to harm people like this, not sure it's common or just really evil and intentional. Again, depending on who it is at times, people will twist it and rationalize it.

Response: AT: *I don't normally comment on the comments of people I don't know, but I agree with your friend, MM. It used to be that "mental illness" was used to describe very serious, debilitating illnesses such as schizophrenia, bipolar, and major depression (just to name a few). To destigmatize mental illness (which I think is a good thing) everything is now included. If you have anxiety, you have a mental illness. Now part of this was also because of health insurance. You have to have a diagnosis in order for insurance to pay... but I digressed. Anyway, because everything under the sun is considered a mental illness, we now are all mentally ill. That waters down the seriousness of the disease, so when "mental illness" is used an excuse, we hear people say, "Well, I know lots of people and they aren't shooting people." It's almost like we need to find a different category: 1) Mentally ill but still able to function in society or 2) mentally ill and needs serious therapy and meds. I'm being facetious. I don't know where common sense falls into this. I think most people know the potential outcomes of walking into a public place and opening fire or parking a truck bomb in front of a building or flying a plane into a building. They know it's wrong, they know they will probably go to jail if they live, and they know there's a good chance they'll die. I just don't think they care. There is so much hate, and I think it is overriding every other thought they have.*

I know this is risky to say, and I know people will disagree with. I've been saying for years that it doesn't matter what's in someone's hands; it's what in their heart. Until we fix the heart, nothing with change. The problem is that fixing the heart is such a HUGE *problem that no one knows how to fix. I don't know how to fix it. I just know that there are some very broken people out there.*

And speaking of broken people, yesterday at work when the Depp/Heard verdict came out, people at work cheered. All I could think of is these are two broken individuals who were in a dysfunctional and toxic relationship. They exposed violence and substance abuse and the worst example of a relationship…and they are both parents. I didn't see anything to cheer. What I saw was tragic.

My response: *Again, I really don't have much to add! I agree with most of what you said! I would like to make a couple of observations.*

DNA... HARDWIRED...

First I think there is a lot of truth to your "facetious" statement about having another category of mental illness. In my book on common sense, I call this the "other" group! Second I agree with the statement about many of us having defective hearts and just being broken human beings in general! I would like to make the following observations though:

o *Seventy percent of mass shootings in developed countries happen in the US.*
o *Americans make up about 4.4 percent of the global population but own 42 percent of the world's guns.*
o *States with lax gun laws tend to have higher rates of violence and deaths related to firearms.*
o *Adjusted for population, only Yemen has a higher rate of mass shootings among countries with more than ten million people. Yemen has the world's second-highest rate of gun ownership after, you guessed it, the United States! Yemen is currently a very dangerous destination for potential travelers. Governments in several countries, including the US, have even issued warnings against traveling to this country for reasons such as terrorism, kidnappings, and other types of violent crime. Visiting Yemen can end in you getting seriously hurt or killed. We should be proud to be in such great company! Now I am being facetious.*
o *A 2015 study estimated that only 4 percent of American gun deaths could be attributed to mental health.*

Countries with the most school shootings:

- *United States: 288*
- *Mexico: eight*
- *South Africa: six*
- *India: five*
- *Nigeria and Pakistan: four*
- *Afghanistan: three*
- *Brazil, Canada, France: two*
- *Azerbaijan, China, Estonia, Germany, Greece, Hungary, Kenya, Russia, and Turkey: one*

So common sense wise, what should these FACTS suggest to us? I am not making a personal judgment, but I think numbers and statistics should at least give us cause for pause on our thoughts on guns and gun control in the good old US of A!

FEELINGS

Could feelings—which is defined as a belief, an emotional state or reaction, especially a vague or irrational one—possibly be the cause of some of us suppressing our common sense in many cases? Yes, in many cases. There are generally seven universally accepted emotions or feelings:

- *Anger*: A strong feeling of annoyance, displeasure, or hostility
- *Fear*: An unpleasant emotion caused by the belief that someone or something is dangerous, likely to cause pain or a threat
- *Disgust:* A feeling of revulsion or strong disapproval aroused by something unpleasant or offensive
- *Happiness*: A statement of well-being and contentment, joy, a pleasurable, or satisfying experience
- *Sadness*: Emotional pain associated with or characterized by feelings of disadvantage
- *Loss*: Despair, surprise, an unexpected or astonishing event, fact, or thing
- *Contempt*: The feeling that a person or a thing is beneath consideration, worthless, or deserving scorn

Out of these seven generally universally accepted emotions or feelings, notice that only one, happiness, has a positive tone to it. Do we ever react due to any of these or other feelings? Yes, many times! Are these reactions normally based on reasoning, logic, or common sense? Usually not! Reread the definition of feelings, "A belief, an emotional state, or reaction, especially a *vague* or *irrational* one!" Feeling love for a lover is one of those areas that sometimes has us questioning one's common sense. Many times, outside observers wonder why an individual would allow themselves to be subjected to the repeated and ongoing abuse in a relationship from someone who proclaims to love them. It just doesn't seem to make much common sense to us! I know there are many who study human behavior who have many reasons why this occurs, but I would suspect these reasons aren't based on intelligence, logic, or common sense!

Observation: I have a Black/Afro-American female friend. She is a lot younger than me. She is approximately thirty-nine years of age. She is young enough to be my daughter. I have known her for approximately fourteen or fifteen years or so. I have always considered her to be very intelligent and possess a healthy dose of common sense! She attained her master's degree at approximately the young age of twenty-two years old. She presently owns two successful businesses she started on her own. Approximately thirteen or fourteen years ago, she met and married her husband. He is Caucasian. They have children together; their children are biracial. He is a racist. She knew this before marrying him. He uses the word nigger in her presence, and I am assuming he has used the word nigger in the presence of their biracial children. He frequently talks about Blacks in a derogatory, disrespectful, and degrading manner. He knows I am a friend of hers, and she has told me that he has referred to me as a nigger.

> June 6–12, 2022 (social medial post): *As I have previously stated, I like to use real-life examples to illustrate some of my points. The following is an example that relates to both our topics of discussion on relationships and common sense in connection to the feeling of love! I know this young twenty-five–forty-five-year-old Afro-American. I can verify that they are very intelligent and did not have any problems earning a master's degree in college before the age of twenty-five! Some years ago, they met and married their mate who is Caucasian. They*

have at least one biracial child together. Their mate is a racist and does not like Black people! They frequently talk about Afro-Americans in a very disrespectful and derogatory manner! They freely use the word nigger when speaking of Afro-Americans! They use the term in the presence of their mate and children! The Afro-American knew of their mate's racism prior to marriage! Is it possible that this is an example of where feelings of love are exemplified as an emotional state or reaction, especially a vague or irrational one, and possibly be causing both to suppress their logic and common sense for what they view as love for one another?

Response: AT: *I thought about this all weekend. I'm going to look at this as I would a situation of emotional abuse because that's what I think it is. The fact that race is involved makes it more emotional, but it's still abuse. I'm also going to give them names and sexes because I need it to organize my thoughts. I do recognize I'm being a little stereotypical here, but again, my brain needs a way to organize my thoughts, so here it goes. I'm not surprised "Sue," who I'm calling the African American, married "Bob," who I'm calling the Caucasian. We see this all the time. We ignore red flags. We think they didn't really mean it; it's not that bad; they have so many other great traits; they'll change; I can change them; they'll change when we get married; they'll change when we have kids, on and on. We excuse bad behavior all the time in the name of love. We tolerate things from those we love that we wouldn't from others.*

What surprises me is why "Bob" married "Sue." For example, I know a man who hates women. All women. But of course, he has a wife. He has to have a wife because who else is going to wait on him and give him children. So he has to tolerate women to get what he wants. But if "Bob" doesn't like a certain race (sees them as lesser than), then why marry that race? There are plenty others to choose from. This seems like a sadistic behavior. Purposely marrying someone you view as lesser than and having a child that you see as lesser than. What parent doesn't think their child hung the moon? That almost sounds pathological. That is bizarre behavior, and I don't understand, but I'm not sure love is involved and/or suppressing anything. But not to be totally anti-"Bob." I think "Bob" needs some serious therapy to figure out what's going on. Most people run from the fire, not into the fire.

My response: *I agree with your thoughts on why Sue may have married Bob! As far as why Bob may have married Sue? If you can understand why a man who hates women might marry a woman he hates, then I suspect the same logic or reasoning, or lack of, might follow for someone marrying someone of a race they hate! I honestly don't know why Bob married into a race he hates and has biracial children as a result of that marriage! I only cited the case to illustrate how we as human beings sometimes do things that just don't seem to make much common sense! It would be interesting to have Bob share his reasoning(s) for doing what he did, or maybe someone else in this discussion can share their thoughts…*

Response: AT: *People are icebergs.*

DNA... HARDWIRED...

> My response: *Lol! I find comfort in the fact that there are far more people out there that are like you and I with big warm hearts that can melt those icebergs!*

Remember the definition of common sense, "Common knowledge that most people (except babies and those with mental challenges) should know!" As I stated previously, I consider her to be very intelligent and possess a healthy dose of common sense. She is not a baby, and she does not have any mental challenges that I am aware of! It is very obvious to me that she falls into the category that is not a baby, mentally challenged, or most people! She, and I will assume he, are in the category I am most interested in, "the other!"

> June 6–12, 2022 (social medial post): *This week's common sense topic of discussion is, could feelings—which are defined as a belief, an emotional state, or reaction, especially a vague or irrational one—possibly be the cause of some of us suppressing our common sense in many cases?*
>
> Response: AT: *Absolutely! I totally believe it's our feelings that drive our actions, even when sometimes those actions seem to go against common sense. I think the two strongest emotional drivers are loss and fear. Side note: many people would say anger because we see anger manifest all around us. But if you slide anger out of the way (like a patio door), what's behind it? Loss and fear. When a person goes to counseling, what are the common reasons? Loss of a relationship, loss of a loved one, loss of a job, loss of an identity, loss of friendship, etc. We don't like to lose things; it hurts. Watch the news; we see groups of people who are motivated by the fear of a loss: identity, security, culture, free-*

dom, etc. The loss doesn't even have to happen yet; it can be the fear of a potential loss. So back to my original statement, I think loss and fear are our emotional drivers. If those are strong enough, they can convince us to do things which we might not ordinarily do…or in other words, ignore common sense.

RELIGION

Webster defines religion as the belief in a god or belief in a group of gods. An organized system of beliefs, ceremonies, rituals, and rules is used to worship a god or a group of gods. An interest, a belief, or an activity that is very important to a person or group relating to or manifesting faithful devotion to an acknowledged ultimate reality or deity!

It is believed that man first came into existence 1.4 million to 2.4 million years ago… The Bible is estimated to have been written approximately two thousand years ago… No point to be made…I just found it interesting that there is a possible one million-year difference in the estimated time man came into existence and that the Bible was written as recent as approximately two thousand years ago… Those who believe in evolution *and* the Bible must have a very difficult time resolving the obvious conflict there is between the Bible and man's existence or evolution…

The practice of religion, in general, is usually good and positive for all! It improves health, learning, economic well-being, self-control, self-esteem, and empathy! There are some cases where religion is not positive but negative, i.e., suppressing human sexuality, silencing and oppressing women, teaching people not to question things, history of resisting the development of science, etc.

I am sure most will agree that religion is primarily based on faith and, many cases, a very strong faith! What is faith? It is a complete trust or confidence in someone or something, most times sight unseen! It is also a strong belief in God or the doctrines of a religion based on spiritual apprehension rather than proof! Many will not agree, but generally, religion or one's faith is not based in fact, or some would say, nor is it based on common sense! There are many types of religions, beliefs, and faiths! Which is truly the correct one? Whose god is the real or correct god? I would suspect that all true believers of different faiths believe their god and religion is the real or correct one! Common sense would say that all religions and faiths can't be universally correct since there are so many differences in many cases! Strictly from a faith, belief, or psychological view, religion, and multiple gods are reasonable to the believers, but it shouldn't be expected to be reasonable or make common sense to the nonbeliever or outside observer! I do believe there is a creator, a god, a superior being, but I, like everyone else, can only guess what that looks like since I nor anyone else has ever personally seen or audibly heard their god!

Someone suggested to me that some people believe they have seen or heard their god. I can only remind that person that this is a book on common sense, "sound and prudent judgment based on a simple perception of the situation or facts shared by *nearly* all people except babies and those with mental challenges!" I doubt that nearly all people except babies and those with mental challenges would believe that there are those who have truly seen or talked to God!

In the year 2021, the majority of Republicans say they still believe Donald Trump won the 2020 US presidential election according to a Reuters/Ipsos opinion poll. The poll found that 53 percent of Republicans, 3 percent of Democrats, and 25 percent of all Americans say they believe that Donald Trump is the true president of the United States.

I only made the two previous observations to illustrate that when we stray from facts or common sense, we can end up in some very dark and strange places!

What are the two major religions in the world? They are Christianity and Islam! There are many others, but those are said to be the most prevalent ones! I will not attempt to teach or instruct you on either of these faiths or religions or say which is right or wrong since I don't personally know, but I would like to discuss some of the important aspects and see the role common sense plays in religion…or not! I will say that I do believe they both have a positive foundation and promote positive teachings on how we should

DNA... HARDWIRED...

treat our fellow man and live our lives! They also both have some believers that take their interpretations to a violent and unhealthy extreme. They are based on very different beliefs, so they bring the concept of common sense into question and how they can't both be correct.

I find it very interesting that, many times, believers of a particular religion, belief, or faith will bend or manipulate their teachings or beliefs to suit a particular situation. Many times, they are very hypocritical. In the four years of Pres. Donald Trump's presidency, the evangelical right exemplified religious hypocrisy to an art form in the way they all of a sudden were willing to support, promote, and vote for a man who is of very low moral character, corrupt, a notorious liar, incompetent, a narcissist, not a believer or follower of the constitution or rule of law, just to name a few of his moral flaws. Another of the most blatant forms of hypocrisy I have seen in the Christian faith is not judging others. Matthew 7:1–2 Jesus says, "Judge not or you too will be judged. For in the same way, you judge others, you will be judged, and with the measure you use, it will be measured to you!" We are all judgmental at times, but in my personal experience, Christians in general are one of the most judgmental groups of people I have ever encountered! They even use the teaching of their religion to try and justify their judging!

Christianity is defined as "the religion based on the person and teachings of Jesus of Nazareth or its beliefs and practices!" There are thousands of separate churches, sects, and denominations that make up the modern Christian tradition, but they all seem to be based on the foundation and teachings of the Bible. The Bible is defined as the Christian scriptures, consisting of the Old and New testaments. There are also the Jewish scriptures, consisting of the Torah or Law, the Prophets, and the Hagiographa or Writings. The Bible consists of many scriptures that are often interrupted differently by teachers and followers of the Christian faith. Common sense would say that man wrote the Bible. If this is the case, how can we be assured that man interpreted the instructions and teachings of God or Jesus correctly? Oh, that's right, faith! Faith in whoever is doing the interpreting and teaching of the Bible scriptures! Out of all the teachers of Bible scriptures, I would strongly suspect that there are no two teachers or religious leaders that would interpret and teach on all of the scriptures exactly the same. Common sense would say that is a problem since that indicates a lack of consistency in the interpretation and teaching!

Islam is defined as the religion of the Muslims, a monotheistic faith regarded as revealed through Muhammad as the Prophet of Allah. The Quran is the central religious text of Islam, which Muslims believe to be a revelation from Allah. Again, we are trusting the interpretations and teachings of man.

I will not attempt to teach or instruct on either of these or any other religions since I am not well versed in any of them. I am confident that those who truly believe in and practice these religions are far more knowledgeable than I am, and I am sure they will find fault in my definitions and thoughts on their religions! Religion is one of those subjects in life that many people believe in as much as they believe in science, in many cases, more! Of the two subjects, religion and science, which is more provable or verifiable in most cases? Common sense and science-wise, we all know the answer, but we refuse to acknowledge it out loud! I do strongly believe that mankind has a creator, and God is the designated name for this creator! I also believe generally most well-known and accepted religions are good and are needed in societies for good order and discipline. So I am by no means against religion.

Most traditional religions speak of earth as the only place life or intelligent life exists in the universe. I find this hard to believe… common sense wise. Are we to believe that the creator, God, would create this massive entity called the infinite universe and only put life or intelligent life on this very little, small part of this infinite universe called earth?

DNA... HARDWIRED...

You are here.

Since God is accepted as the creator and all-knowing, it just doesn't make much common sense! I suspect our creator is smart enough to know that we couldn't handle the differences in other life forms since we can't handle the differences in our own human life forms!

I have frequently heard many who believe in God say things like, "Let go. Let God," "If it is God's will then it will be," "Pray on it"... When I hear people say things like that, I often wonder if they are thinking that out of all of the billions of people in the world with many problems they each have, God will stop and take time to resolve each of their own little individual minuscule problems when there is so much more serious and important issues to deal with in the world and the infinite universe? Is this the reason so many of us have difficulties dealing with life's problems, we are waiting on God to solve all? Praying may and often does make us feel better, but one day, we, and all our loved ones, will all die and no amount of praying or leaving it in God's hands will change that! I think one of God's greatest gifts to us human beings, besides life itself, is free will or free choice! It doesn't make much common sense to me for God to give us such a wonderful gift of free will and free choice and then take it away from us without giving us the benefit of learning and growing from our achievements or mistakes. God didn't make us perfect, and even though I haven't talked to God personally, I suspect God doesn't expect us to be perfect. We aren't made to have or ever know all the answers to everything! I believe we can take the collective knowledge of every life form on planet earth, and we will never have or know all the answers to everything!

Observation: Perfect or perfection: "Having all the required or desirable elements, qualities, or characteristics…as good as it gets, absolute, complete!" One of the facts of being human is that *no* one is perfect! This fact appears to get lost on so many of us who choose to judge others as less than perfect based on our thoughts of perfection and our expectations that they meet our thoughts of perfection!

POLITICS

Some common definitions of politics:

- The art or science of government
- The set of activities that are associated with the governance of a country, state, or area. It involves making decisions that apply to groups of members and achieving and exercising positions of governance—organized control over a human community.
- The way that people living in groups make decisions. *Politics* is about making agreements between people so that they can live together in groups such as tribes, cities, or countries.

Observation: I find it very interesting that today there are many who are running for political office but claim they are *not* politicians! They speak of those that are politicians with *disdain*! Politics is a profession just like any other profession and require a degree of knowledge and experience! Would you hire someone to work on your plumbing who claims he is not a plumber? Does that make much common sense? Every voting cycle, millions of Americans vote for celebrities, businesspeople, athletics, etc. for political office with absolutely *no* political knowledge or experience, and they think it is an excellent idea!

Political groups or parties began to form in the United States during the struggle over ratification of the federal constitution of 1787. Friction between parties increased as attention shifted from the creation of a new federal government to the question of how powerful that federal government would be. The Federalists, led by

Secretary of Treasury Alexander Hamilton, wanted a strong central government (present-day Democrats) while the Anti-Federalists (present-day Republicans), led by Secretary of State Thomas Jefferson, advocated states' rights instead of centralized power. Federalists coalesced around the commercial sector of the country while their opponents drew strength from those favoring an agricultural society. The ensuing partisan battles led George Washington to warn of "the baneful effects of the spirit of party" in his farewell address as president of the United States.

"Let me now take a more comprehensive view and warn you in the most solemn manner against the baneful effects of the spirit of party generally" (*George Washington, Farewell Address, September 19, 1796*).

I was very surprised to come across the above quote from George Washington at his farewell address! He adamantly opposed

DNA... HARDWIRED...

and voiced against in the strongest of terms the party system! I have believed and felt for the longest time that our two-party system doesn't make a whole lot of sense...common sense if you will! Why not? The party system we have in the United States and many other countries of the world is based simply on a team concept! Here in the United States, we have the Republican Party (Conservative) team and the Democratic Party (Liberal) team! I should also mention we have an also-ran team called the Independent Party. They aren't usually well represented and, truthfully, are just discontented members of the Republican or Democratic parties or teams!

Every four years there is a contest where each party selects one person to lead their party or team and the country for the next four years. Usually, these teams do all they can to win, even lie, cheat, and distort the truth about themselves and the other team and the one vying to lead their teams and the country! Winning means everything to these teams! Generally, the voters or "team fans" don't take much interest in finding out what the truth is or not. They just know that for whatever reason, they have chosen a team, and they will vote for their team and leader no matter what, even if they know and feel that their team and/or leader is not good for them overall or the country! Today's politics is a prime example of what Pres. George Washington predicted and warned against!

Originally during the 1860s, the Republicans dominated the northern states orchestrated and promoted programs and policies that supported African Americans. The Democrats dominated the South, opposed these measures, and were against programs and policies that supported African Americans. After the Civil War, Republicans passed laws that granted protections for African Americans and advanced social justice; again, Democrats largely opposed these expansions of power. If at that time, African Americans had the right to vote, common sense wise, which party do you think they would have voted for? I would guess the Republican Party. I would also suspect that White racists or separatists would have voted for the Democratic Party.

At some point in the early to mid-1900s, the parties' philosophies switched. The Democratic Party became the party that supported

African American causes and the Republican Party not so much so. To exemplify this change, Strom Thurmond and George Wallace, were both once Democratic racists and segregationists. Knowing this, if they were alive today, which party do you think they would be members of? Common sense would say the Republican Party. There has been much controversy that the great Civil Rights Leader Martin Luther King was once a registered Republican. If he was alive today, which party do you think he would be affiliated with? Common sense would say the Democratic Party! Hence a question, why are so many African Americans registered Republicans and vote that way today? Knowing the party's history and present-day practices when it comes to race relations, in my mind, it just doesn't make much common sense at all for Blacks and some other minorities to be supportive of the Republican Party! Is it a case of being uninformed about politics or hardwired and therefore a violation of common sense? For me, it is the only thing that even comes close to making any common sense! I have had many discussions with many of my Black Republican family members and friends, and they have yet to offer a reasonable explanation for this phenomenon! I find it interesting that they nor any other Republicans never ask me why I am a Democrat! Common sense wise, I suspect they understand why I would be a Democrat, but they don't seem to be able to apply the same common sense and reasoning to themselves!

So common sense wise, what is the solution to our present situation with our partisan politics? Simple, do away with the teams! No more parties! You run as a person, an individual on your own merit, your own record! This change can't take place overnight. Start at our lowest levels of government or politics. Individuals would start by participating in local politics like local school board, a community organizer, city council, or city commissioner. Move up to mayor and possibly state government like state governor. The next step will be in major politics like congress, the senate, and then possibly the presidency! In all levels of progression, there can be *no* party or group affiliation! You run as the people's candidate! No support from any outside entity! Candidates will be known for their records! Candidates would be provided with the same amount of money from the taxpayers to run their campaigns. Candidates can't use *any* outside money to include their own! Each candidate will get the same amount of marketing time and resources. *No* media outlet can allow just one candidate to advertise through their forum; they have to give *all* candidates the same marketing time and opportunities! There can be *no* marketing of misleading or false truths. This way, no candidate needs to feel or be tempted to only represent a certain group of people or entities!

Observation: In the year 2020, the United States of America had a president named Donald J. Trump, who most intellectually honest people, regardless of party affiliation, would say was a racist, habitual pathological liar, narcissist, and of very low moral character among other poor human qualities! He is the only president in our country's history to ever have been impeached twice! He even led an effort to overthrow our government in the form of an insurrection after his loss for a second term as president of the United States! Without a doubt, he has to be the worst president ever in American history! Most of America and the world know this, but there is a substantial number of Americans who are willing to overlook these flawed and dangerous qualities and are willing to continue supporting him and willing to vote for him for reelection! I suspect they are willing to continue supporting him because politics is a team sport, and they see him as their team leader. This doesn't seem to make a lot of common sense to me!

During Pres. Obama's first term, Republicans promised to do everything they could to block Pres. Obama and make him fail! Senate majority leader at the time, Mitch McConnell, said the single most important thing the Republicans wanted to achieve was to make Pres. Obama a one-term president! Common sense would therefore conclude that if Pres. Obama failed, then so would the country! It is hard to believe that so many American voters would support this agenda, but they did! Not only did they support this agenda, but they also followed through by giving the Republicans both houses the next election! They then, without a doubt, elected the worst president *ever* in American history and was willing to elect him for a second term even after he proved to the world that he was a terrible person and worst president ever in American history! It was amazing that Pres. Obama was still able to get as much accomplished for the people and the country as he did despite the Republicans fighting him every step of the way! Imagine the missed opportunities for the country and its people simply because of our team mentality and racism in our politics!

RACISM

Defined as any attitude, belief, or behavior used to explain and justify prejudice and discrimination against racial or ethnic minorities based on perceived inferiority. If you believe members of a racial group are less intelligent, lazier, or less moral than your racial group, then you are a racist! It is a common thought that people who are racists are ignorant, people who lack knowledge or information! I disagree. I think most of these people are not any more ignorant or lacking any more knowledge than the average person. I still don't have a good or reasonable answer as to what makes a person racist even after all my research. There are many theories like group self-interest, quick to judge others, media representation, racism is taught, etc. None of these or any other reasons explain away an *individual's* apparent ability to choose or not to choose to be racists!

Racial discrimination is described as the unjust or prejudicial treatment of different categories of people, especially on the grounds of their skin color or racial or ethnic origin. It can and often does lead to such issues as discrimination in criminal justice, employment, housing, health care, political power, and education, among other issues. A racist person is a person who commits racist acts. Race is understood by most people as a mixture of physical, behavioral, and cultural characteristics. It is often perceived as something inherent in our biology and therefore inherited across generations. Ethnicity recognizes differences between people mostly based on language and shared culture. It is typically understood as something we acquire, or self-ascribe, based on factors like where we live or the culture we share with others.

Observation: A Caucasian acquaintance/friend once told me that he thought that it was perfectly fine if a small town that consisted all White or Caucasian people did not want or allow Blacks or Afro-Americans to live in their small town! He shared his thoughts and feelings with me in the year 2020! I must admit, I wasn't shocked, but I was surprised that he felt that way and even more surprised that he admitted it to me! Before this, I did have thoughts that he was probably prejudiced, most of us are to a degree, but not racist! Based on his comments, common sense would tell me that he is a racist! I am sure he would not agree with my conclusion, but what else could he be based on the definition of racial discrimination cited above?

There are many who, just like my friend mentioned previously, have these thoughts and feelings on race but don't see themselves as racists or even at least prejudiced! For those of you who may not feel or believe that you are at least prejudiced, ask yourself, how do you feel when you see a Black and White interactional couple? What if the woman is Black and the man is White? What if the man is Black and the woman is White? What if the woman is White and the man is of a race other than Black? What are your thoughts on your White daughter dating or marrying a Black man? Did your thoughts and feelings change depending on the couple's sex and race? Chances are, with many of you, your thoughts and feelings did change, but you won't acknowledge or admit it!

Our judicial system is inundated with cases and examples of injustices brought upon Afro-Americans and People of Color! If we can't rely on our judicial system to apply equal justice to all our citizens, and it is their job to apply equal justice to us all, how can we expect the average citizen to not be tainted with a degree of prejudice or racism? Our justice system is supposed to depend on equal treatment and investigations based on evidence, not stereotypes or bias. America talks about the ideals of equality and opportunity for all, but we have never lived up to those ideals and dreams in all cases. Some of us face more barriers than others in achieving these ideals because of who we are, what we look like, or where we come from. People are frequently heard saying, "I don't see color. I judge people based on who they are!" Common sense says that we all see color unless we are truly colorblind, and even then there are other physical characteristics that we see that indicate our race. So if I can't trust

DNA... HARDWIRED...

you to be honest and admit that you do see one's color, how can I trust you to be honest and admit how you truly feel about People of Color? Do racists know that they are racists? How can they not know? Do racists choose to be racists? How is it not a choice? Is it in their DNA? Are they hardwired to be racist? Why are there some people who were raised in a racist environment but aren't racists? Why are there some people who were not raised in a racist environment but are now racists? Does it make common sense for one to be racists? Self-reflection...are you racists?

Observation: Black Lives Matter (BLM), an international social movement formed in the United States in 2013, is dedicated to fighting racism and anti-Black violence, especially in the form of police brutality! Why does this term and social movement cause so much anger and division among the races? History shows that when White people feel threatened by social justice movements, like BLM and the equal rights movements of the '60s, they lash out. Don't be misguided, the lashing out is driven by hate, resentment, fear, and racism, not reasoning, logic, or common sense!

> May 20–26, 2022 (social medial post): *I suspect that we didn't change many people's minds on their politics last week! Hopefully, we can agree that no matter our political party affiliation, we are Americans and want America to be successful!*
>
> *This week's common sense discussion topic is probably the most hated topic people don't like to talk about, racism! Racism is defined as any attitude, belief, or behavior used to explain and justify prejudice and discrimination against racial or ethnic minorities, based on perceived inferiority! If you believe members of a racial group are less intelligent, lazier, less moral, or in other ways lesser than your racial group, then you are a racist! It is a common thought that people who are racists are ignorant*

people who lack knowledge or information! I disagree. I think most of these people are not any more ignorant or lack any more knowledge than the average person! I still don't have a good or reasonable answer as to what makes a person racist even after all my research. There are many theories like group self-interest, quickness to judge others, media representation, racism is taught, etc. None of these or any other reasons explain away an individual's apparent ability to choose or not to choose to be racists! I know I have friends who are racists, but I suspect they don't know they are! A White acquaintance/ friend, who I would consider being professional and intelligent, once suggested to me that they thought it would be perfectly fine if a small town of Whites only wanted to exclude anyone of another race from living in that town! Now those of you that know me, you know I have been on this earth for a few years, and based on what I just shared, you might think this happened down South back in the '60s or '70s! No, this happened in 2021 in Phoenix, Arizona! Many of you might think this upset me, and I went off on this individual! No, it didn't upset me, and I didn't go off on this person! If I had reacted that way, I would have been extremely disappointed in myself for being so naïve and unaware that there are racists that still exist even in 2021! Truthfully, I sincerely believe this individual doesn't realize they are a racist! In my mind, they didn't fit the description of who we typically view as a racist prior to this incident!

I am still encouraging feedback from everyone, but please continue to remain

DNA... HARDWIRED...

respectful with your comments! I know this is a hot topic and feelings can run deep and are sometimes raw!

Response: LC: *James, I will start by saying, you and your daughter have taught me so much! You are one of the few with whom I feel comfortable discussing hot topics. I always thought I had a grasp on racism. Now I feel I only know how much I have to learn. Racism is so much more than an offhand remark or joke. To me, it's such a huge problem and yet such a simple concept. People try to make themselves feel better or worth more by thinking less of others. Like you said, usually while loudly proclaiming they're not racist they have this friend! It's ridiculous.*

My response: *LC, thank you for giving me and Nickie credit for your learning about racism, but please know that you are responsible for your awareness and growth! Without you being willing to be open to learning about hot topics, learning would not occur! Nickie and I have always loved and appreciated that about you! I agree with all that you said about racism! Especially the part about racism being such a huge problem, but the concept of not being racist is such a simple concept! Hopefully, with these discussions, there will be more who will be open to hot topic discussions and become aware...*

Response: AT: *You aren't shying away, are you? Truthfully, I think all the -isms (race, gender, age, religion, culture, etc.) are destructive and unhealthy. I also think they are very, very complicated. It's not one cause or one reason; it's a combination of them all intertwined together and different for different people, which is why it's so hard to overcome. I also think part of the problem is there are different definitions.*

A couple of stories: 1) Almost thirty years ago in Georgia, a friend of mine (Black) was telling me about a fight she got into with her husband (Black). They were in their car and stopped at a red light in an older part of town. There were several men standing on the street corner (all Black). She reached over and locked her door (remember when we used to have to manually push down the button). Her husband immediately started calling her a racist. I think she felt unsafe and wanted to make herself feel safe. She is still my friend, and I would never call her a racist. 2) About twelve years ago, I was in a staff meeting telling my coworkers about an army officer who was put on the do not give AF Aid to list because he was removing the ink from their checks and writing in new amounts. I never mentioned a race and his name didn't give it away. As I was telling the story about him being confronted by the bank and his leadership, I mentioned he keeps lying. I said, "He keeps hanging himself." A coworker (Hispanic) filed a report that I made a racist statement. My boss and my boss's boss (both Black) were in the room when I said it, and both supported me. 3) A few years ago, we went to South Dakota and toured the Indian University and the Crazy Horse Memorial. When we were there, the Indian tour guides said they prefer the term Indian, referred to themselves as Indian, and asked us to refer to them as Indians. They were also very proud of the university, which is called the Indian University of North America. About a month ago at work, I was telling my coworkers about our trip to South Dakota and about this beautiful school and immediately a woman (White) said I was being racist.

Again, I don't think we're all working with the same definitions. Sometimes it feels like one can't win for losing. No matter what, someone is upset or offended. You just can't make everyone happy. The older I get, the less I try. Another person's (fill in the blank) is not a threat to my own. I just try to do the best I can. I'm going to make mistakes from time to time because I'm human. But I know what's in my heart and so does God.

My response: *I agree that racism can be and often is very complicated, but with knowledge, understanding, and communication, it can be a lot less complicated! You also brought up a good point about definitions! I think we frequently get the terms racism and prejudice mixed up many times! Prejudice is more of a hostile or dismissive general attitude, thought, or feeling toward a race that is usually different from ours! It usually comes out of not investigating the facts and not knowing the true nature of whatever the thing is we are prejudiced against! In most cases, it is irrational and a case of stereotypes and ignorance! I suspect that the incidents you shared would be more of a case of prejudice, if anything, rather than racism if the incidents did have any merit! I would dare to guess that many of us have prejudices toward other races and sometimes even our own race as you illustrated with the example of the Black wife locking the door in the Black neighborhood! We can also have a prejudice about many things other than one's race even though race is what we mostly identify the term with! Racism, on the other hand, is a set of beliefs that one color or race is better than another which justifies those attitudes, thoughts, or feelings and makes the case for some sort of action of discrimination or inequality! Racism can also exist when people are mistreated or treated unfairly based on their race!*

There are other words and definitions dealing with race that can cause us problems, and you also touched on that! Again, I just think it is a simple matter of effective communication and being sensitive to others and their feelings which can bring about awareness and understanding! For example, what term is preferred for the Black race today? We came from being called Colored, Negro, Black to Afro-American! Would the use of any of those names or terms be considered prejudice or racist today? What about Blacks that immigrated to this country after slavery from other countries other than the continent of Africa? Should they be addressed as Colored, Negro, Black, or Afro-American? How would they prefer to be addressed? Are they offended because they are automatically thrown into the Afro-American pot? What about folks that immigrated from other countries and look like they are American-born Caucasians? What about the following terms: Indian, Indian giver, squaw, gyp or gip, jerry-rigged, peanut gallery, uppity, paddy wagon, bugger, Houlihan, jap,

DNA... HARDWIRED...

> *wop, etc., are they racist terms? I would suggest that maybe we should just play it safe and not use any derogatory terms or terms we don't know the meaning of toward any race or people! I think we can usually determine if a person intended to be insulting or if it was just an honest case of ignorance! Please don't give up! It is going to take us all to try and help bring us all together...* ♥ *Thoughts?*

Response: LC: *AT, well said.*

Response: LC: *James, again, I agree. In my attempts to be respectful, I've gotten it wrong twice. 1) While working at a wildlife park on a reservation, I was meeting with a native man looking for feathers. I made reference to the specific community he was representing (Salt River/Pima Indian Reservation) and was immediately uncomfortable. Did I just insult him? So I asked, "What is your preference?" He thanked me for being kind and open to learning. I was told few natives people's hate the term Indian. Most hate the way it is said. We talked for over an hour. I learned so much from him. 2) I referred to a young friend of my daughter's as Latin American. She laughed. She told me, while she appreciates the effort, she was Mexican and proud of it. Again, Mexican wasn't the slur. It is always about how the word is said. I have found over the years the fastest way to the correct information is going to the source. I always ask first if they are open to a question about their culture/race/sexuality. I have found people more than willing to explain a topic if I simply start with respect. And now I need to go look up why paddy wagon and bugger are wrong...*

but I knew about the rest. I don't use them, and heaven help someone who uses derogatory terms in front of me.

My response: *LC, again, it's all about effectively communicating and having a desire to be respectful of others! There are too many people like the lady I posted a picture of with the red shirt on that let everyone know that she didn't care about their feelings! Thank you for caring!* ♥

RELATIONSHIPS

Defined as how two or more people are connected and relate to each other! There are many types of relationships. Five of the most common ones are listed below. These are not the only types of relationships, just the most common. There are some common indicators of a good or bad relationship.

Dating relationship: A stage of a romantic relationship in humans whereby two people meet socially with the aim of each assessing the other's suitability as a prospective partner in an intimate relationship. It is a form of courtship consisting of social activities done by the couple, either alone or with others. People date for many reasons: companionship, fun, sex, intimacy, socialization, helping you find the right mate, prepare for marriage, etc. It would probably be wise to determine what kind of relationship one is looking for at the beginning of the relationship if we hope or want the relationship to succeed. Many times, dating relationships fail due to different desires or goals for the relationship and people not being honest upfront. Dating is the stage in a romantic relationship where the decision to move to the next step, marriage, is usually decided. Common sense wise, the high divorce rate of one out of every two marriages ending in divorce would indicate that we don't do a very good job of assessing our suitability for a lifelong partner before marriage. I would also speculate that out of the marriages that don't end in divorce, there is undoubtedly a large number that should not be considered as successful marriages. There are many marriages that are failures due to their dysfunction, thus increasing the actual number of failed marriages substantially!

There are five stages to dating:

1. *Attraction:* This is the first stage in dating and usually determines if the relationship will develop into something more. There has to be an attraction in order for the relationship to develop into something romantic. This is the stage where everything seems new and exciting! This stage usually lasts a few months. There is usually a lot of contact consisting of phone calls, texting, many dates, etc. to help a couple decide if they will move to the next stage.
2. *Reality:* This stage usually creeps up on the couple and may last a few months. This is the stage where the couple may start to see faults in each other. This doesn't mean you no longer like each other, but reality sets in after that initial attraction wears off. You may begin to see little habits or behaviors that you didn't notice in the attraction stage, and it bothers you. This is the stage where many relationships fail. Common sense would indicate that if the couple is noticing some behaviors or habits that are raising red flags, then maybe the relationship should fail at this stage. The high divorce rate indicates that common sense is not followed in many cases at this stage.
3. *Commitment:* If you make it past the reality stage, you enter the commitment stage. At this point, the couple have decided to date each other exclusively. They are aware of the flaws in each other and are willing to accept those flaws as part of the person. Again, common sense is not applied many times in this stage.
4. *Intimacy:* Stage four is intimacy and usually occurs months after love has been growing for the couple. This stage isn't just physical intimacy but much deeper into the realm of truly bonding with each other and true love. This stage usually means opening up to each other and letting your guards down.

DNA... HARDWIRED...

5. *Engagement:* This is the stage where the couple has decided to commit to a lifelong partnership and future together in marriage.

Observation: Through my research and life's observations, I have determined that if a woman is single at the age of forty and up and not in a serious relationship that is destined for marriage in the near future, she will probably not meet and marry an eligible man unless one of the following occur:

- She meets a recently divorced eligible man
- She meets a recently widowed eligible man
- She takes an eligible married man from his wife

I am sure that there will be many that will not understand or agree with my observation above, so let me try and explain how and why I have reached the conclusion I have.

First the following are some qualities of what I would consider an *eligible* man possesses:

- Attractive
- Financially secure
- He is giving
- Personable
- Respects you
- Shares your values
- Honest
- Sincere
- Sense of humor
- Effective commutator, he listens
- Supports your career
- Thoughtful and romantic
- Spends time with you

So, ladies, if you agree with *half* of the qualities of a good man I cited above, write down the names of three *single* heterosexual men that are over forty years of age that you know that is not recently divorced or widowed that would meet those qualities! Wait, I will make it easier for you. Get with some of your other girlfriends and, *together*, come up with three names.

Second to my surprise, men are more likely to be single today than women! I initially thought that the reason women were having such a difficult time finding a mate was due to there being a lot more single women than single men! Not so. There are more single men! Much of this phenomenon has to do with the fact that there aren't as many "eligible" men available today! Almost a third of adult single men live with a parent. Single men are much more likely to be unemployed, financially fragile, and lack a degree than those with a partner! They are also likely to have lower median income. Single men earned less in 2019 than in 1990. Single women earn the same as they did thirty years ago, and those with partners have increased their earnings by 50 percent.

Marital relationship: The relationship between wife and husband. It is estimated that approximately 50 percent of all first marriages fail and end in divorce. The total number of marriages that fail, including those that don't end in divorce, is much higher than 50 percent. In other words, many marriages are failures but don't end in divorce. Most couples stay in failed marriages due to fear! Fear of the unknown, being alone, children, financial, change, etc., but fear is usually at the root of it all! Most marriages can succeed if couples just realize the following:

- Make marriage the priority
- Maintain an open line of communication
- Focus on each other's strengths rather than weaknesses, don't try to change each other
- Don't focus on small things
- Don't let others interfere in your relationship
- Accept and realize there will probably be change in each other and the relationship over time…adapt
- Compliment rather than complain, support each other
- Maintain respect for each other, trust each other

- Accept and appreciate each other…don't take each other for granted
- Continue to do things to attract each other
- Spend quality time together

Observation: It has been said that Albert Einstein once said, *"Women marry men hoping they will change. Men marry women hoping they will not. So each is inevitably disappointed!"*

Based on the odds against finding an eligible man over forty, I would suggest you ladies do everything possible to stay with the man you are with, and you and he try to work on those areas that require work an improvement.

Friendship relationship: A friend is a person with whom one has a bond of mutual affection or love, typically excluding sexual or family relations. Some positive qualities of a good friend are honesty, trustworthiness, dependability, loyalty, nonjudgmental, and being a good listener. There are varying degrees of friendship: casual, close, and very close. The different degrees of friendship require different degrees of commitment and expectations for the relationship. It is important to understand the type of friendship you have.

Observation: A common mistake that men and women make in man-and-woman friendship relationships is thinking the friendship can remain platonic. It is very rare for a heterosexual male to only see his woman friend as a friend and not see her in a sexual way. He may try not to appear as though he wants more than a platonic friendship, but most heterosexual men do not want to play the role of a woman's gay boyfriend!

Family relationship: Members related by birth, marriage, or adoption. Includes immediate and extended family members. In a healthy family, members trust and rely on each other for support, love, affection, and warmth. Members share common goals and work together to reach those goals. Family relationships are more likely to be lifelong.

Work relationship: The relationship between people who interact because of their work. Unlike the previous types of relationships mentioned, a sense of caring or love for those involved is not required.

What is required is effective communication, respect, trust, a sense of diversity, and empathy. Many times, friendship and dating relationships develop as a result of a working relationship. Many times, problems develop as a result of mixing work relationships with other relationships.

Many of us seek all types of relationship counseling to help solve our relationship problems. Counseling is defined as "assistance and guidance in resolving personal, social, or psychological problems and difficulties and involves helping people make changes in ways of thinking, feeling, or acting, especially by a professional." The concept of counseling and its general results further convinces me that we are hardwired in many ways, and common sense won't overcome that fact. Let's assume that most professional counselors are knowledgeable, well trained, and experienced. The odds are that most professional, knowledgeable, well trained, and experienced counselors can determine what the cause or causes of discord are in a relationship after a few counseling sessions with the parties involved. Problem solved and case closed, right? No, not really. Counselors don't typically just tell parties what they think the problem is, who may be at fault, and what to do to correct the problem. They try to help those in counseling come to those conclusions on their own with the counselor's help and guidance. When this occurs, we can be assured the parties truly do "get it"! The problem is, just like with most situations dealing with differences of opinions, thoughts, and perceptions, it's very hard, if not impossible, for someone to overcome the power of being hardwired in a particular way of thinking and acting, even with the assistance of a professional therapist or counselor!

Observation: The same people who will go to a professionally trained and qualified counselor for assistance with a relationship or other problem and not take the counselor's advice or guidance are the same people who will go to a professionally trained and qualified plumber and follow their diagnosis and follow their advance or guidance! What makes the advance or guidance given by the professionally trained and qualified plumber more credible than the advance or guidance given by the professionally trained qualified counselor?

DNA... HARDWIRED...

Observation: There are usually givers and takers in any relationship. The "sweet spot" is for the giver and taker to be as close to the center as possible. In other words, we don't want the giver giving too much and the taker taking too much! It upsets the balance. It is very common in a relationship for the parties not to be aware of whether they are a giver or taker resulting in an imbalance in the relationship. What can be worse is for takers to think they are givers. Givers don't normally see themselves as takers. They are fully aware they are givers and, many times, feel they are taken advantage of by takers. A sign of whether or not you are a giver or a taker is takers say no a lot and givers say yes a lot to reasonable requests in relationships.

COMMUNICATION

Simply put, communication is the act of transferring information from one place, person, or group to another. Every act of communication involves at least one sender, a message, means of transmission, and a recipient. Sounds pretty straightforward, right? No, not so fast! We all need to communicate and should want our communication to be understood and effective, but there are many barriers to *effective* communication. Not actively listening, not being clear and concise, not caring about the concerns of others, not being honest and transparent, having preconceived thoughts and feelings, wanting to be right, being defensive, shutting down are just a few of the most common barriers to effective communication. Let's look at these barriers individually and see the role common sense, or lack thereof, plays in each:

- *Not actively listening:* Active listening is the process of listening attentively and listening positively. If all parties in a communicating process are not listening attentively and listening positively, then you are not actively listening, and the communication process you are involved in will most likely fail and not be effective! Active listening is a skill, and it takes practice in most cases. Many times, we think we are actively listening, but really, we are just hearing what the other person is saying and thinking of an answer to give to their point when it is our turn to respond. Remember, active listening is a process that requires being attentive and positive.
- *Not being clear and concise:* When you are communicating with someone and trying to make a point, giving them

too much information and not being clear and concise can make it harder for them to know what is most important. With fewer words, your listener has an easier time separating what is important and what is not! When you are clear and concise when speaking, you will get straight to your point in a way those you are speaking to can easily understand and comprehend.

- *Not caring about the concerns of others:* Communication should be a two-way process! The other person's thoughts and feelings are as important as your own. We need to have that give-and-take attitude when communicating. Asking clarifying questions and letting the other person know we are listening is an excellent way to show that we care about them and what they have to say!
- *Not being honest and transparent:* Honest and transparent communication builds trust. Without trust, relationships can't grow! The amount of transparency you provide should be in direct relation to how much trust you have for the person. It is a complicated and delicate process! You need trust to feel comfortable enough to be transparent; at the same time, you need transparency if you hope to deepen your trust levels. The length of time you have been in a relationship with someone doesn't necessarily determine the amount of trust you do or do not have for that person. Someone who has been in a relationship for a year may have more trust for their partner than someone who has been in a relationship with their partner for thirty years! It all comes down to how safe a person feels in a relationship at any given moment. If you don't feel safe, you won't be transparent!
- *Preconceived thoughts and feelings:* Words are intangible thoughts of the mind. Many think of words as concrete ideas that are completely objective. This is not the case. People identify with different ideas based on their own experience and knowledge. Therefore, their perception of common ideas or words may differ radically based on

experience, culture, and language. You can see how preconceived thoughts and feelings can greatly affect the communication process.
- *Wanting to be right:* Effective communication is not a competition. Being right is not effective communication. No one wants to live or work with a person who is always right. It makes others feel inferior and they will likely withdraw from you.
- *Being defensive:* Defensiveness and effective communication do not go together. Defensiveness will quickly end open and effective communication. Many times, one party in a conversation acts defensive which causes the other party to react defensively and so on and so on.
- *Shutting down:* Shutting down means you are refusing to continue a discussion to avoid discussing a disagreement and dismissing others' concerns. This usually results in intensified emotions to include anger and more complexity in the relationship.

One day, I was at my gym working out. I was working out on a piece of equipment called a Universal Workout Machine. In a commercial gym, the Universal Workout Machine is a piece of gym equipment that is connected by a group of workstations. This particular Universal Workout Machine had four different connected workout pieces of workout equipment. I was using one piece of equipment, a young man was using another piece of equipment, and a young lady was using another piece of equipment at an end workstation. The young man was to my right, and the young lady was to his right and directly across facing me. The equipment the young man was using required two small removable handles. The handles he had weren't a match, so he decided to go and find another matching handle. As he was walking away, he could see the young lady eying his piece of equipment and saw her walk over and take the one handle he had left on the equipment he was using. I could tell that she thought he was done with the equipment and was not coming back to it. So now I am watching him find *two* matching handles for his piece of equipment. After he found two matching handles, he returned to his equipment to the surprise of the young lady. As I am watching this uncomfortable situation for the two of them play out, I couldn't help but find it very amusing!

He was giving her the "stink eye," and she was trying to avoid making eye contact with him after now realizing she had taken his handle. After watching this play out for five to ten minutes, I decided to intervene. I asked them both if I could show them something, and they both said yes, sure. I asked the young lady did she realize she had taken the young man's handle, and she said yes but not at the time she was taking it. I asked her when she took the handle, did she think he was returning to the equipment, and she said no, she thought he was done. I asked him, "Did you see her take your handle?" And he said yes. I asked him did he think she realized at the time that he wasn't done with the equipment, and he said he wasn't sure, but he didn't think she realized he was still using the equipment. I asked if they were both feeling uncomfortable and stressed about the incident, and they both said yes.

So I asked her, "What do you think you should have said to him after realizing you had taken his handle?"

She said, "I should have asked him if he was still using that handle."

I asked him, "And what would your response have been?"

He said, "I would have said yes, but it was okay."

I asked her, "What would your response have been to him?"

She said, "I would have told him I was sorry, and I didn't realize he wasn't done."

I asked him then, "What would your response have been?"

"I would have told her it was okay. I now realize it was a mistake, and she didn't realize I wasn't done."

So at that point, I suggested they both introduce themselves to each other, exchange phone numbers, start dating, get married, have kids, and live happily ever after. We all had a good laugh, and the unnecessary stressful and tense situation was gone.

In the above situation, they both knew what they should have said and should have done, but neither was willing or understood how to take the necessary step of communicating in a clear and precise manner to clarify a very obvious case of misunderstanding! This situation occurs daily with us and people we know and don't know.

PARENTING

Simply put, parenting is the activity of bringing up a child as a parent! Just like most of our life lessons, we aren't formally taught how to be a good parent or even how to parent at all! We don't take parenting classes usually unless they are ordered by the authorities due to some incident or incidents that indicate that we probably need the classes due to our poor parenting skills! We usually learn how to parent from observing how others parent, usually our parents. If we believe they did a good job parenting, then we will probably attempt to parent the way they did. If we believe they did a bad job parenting, then we probably attempt to avoid parenting the way they did. One of the problems with this thought process is that we could be wrong on both counts. Maybe our parents were terrible parents, but we thought they were great parents! So we parent the way they did, and our kids turn out terrible, and we can't understand why it could be the opposite. Maybe our parents were great parents, but we didn't think so, so we parent differently than they did, and our kids turn out terrible, and we can't understand why! The truth is, we will probably parent the way our parents did in some ways whether they were good or bad parents! That is why I said, attempt! Parents are usually not all good or all bad at parenting, so hopefully, we are using the good parenting techniques we learned from our parents.

It is said that parenting styles generally fall into four accepted broad categories. Though different researchers give different names to them, the styles usually are said to be *authoritarian*, *authoritative*, *permissive*, and *uninvolved*.

- *Authoritarian:* Characterized by high demands and low responsiveness. Parents with an *authoritarian style* of par-

enting have very high expectations of their children yet provide very little in the way of feedback and nurturance. Mistakes tend to be punished harshly.
- *Authoritative:* Characterized by high responsiveness and high demands. *Authoritative* parents are responsive to the child's emotional needs while having high standards. They set limits and are very consistent in enforcing boundaries.
- *Permissive:* Permissive parenting is a type of parenting style characterized by low demands with high responsiveness. Permissive parents tend to be very loving yet provide few guidelines and rules. These parents do not expect mature *behavior* from their children and often seem more like a friend than parental figures.
- *Uninvolved:* Sometimes referred to as neglectful *parenting*, is a *style* characterized by a lack of responsiveness to a child's needs. *Uninvolved* parents make few to no demands of their children, and they are often indifferent, dismissive, or even completely neglectful.

If you agree that the four categories above are generally the accepted parenting styles common sense wise, which one would probably be the most effective one? If you are a parent, which type of parent are you? Do you believe you need and should make some adjustments to your parenting styles? Chances are most people will see the need to make some adjustments to their parenting styles but won't! I believe this is a case where many individuals being "hardwired" will affect their abilities to use common sense and make the necessary adjustments. This is a perfect opportunity for you to determine if what I have been trying to share with you in this book is making sense…or common sense!

Observation: One of the most common problems I see with parents raising kids is parents seem to think that in the first few years of a child's life, they don't need parenting in the form of responding to a child's emotional needs while setting high standards. Parents don't set limits and aren't very consistent in enforcing boundaries. They don't seem to realize that the first few years of a child's life is probably without a doubt the most important time for setting standards of discipline and establishing a foundation structure for the rest of their growing life! It is thought by most experts in child development that a child's personality starts to develop within the first few months of life but makes most gains of development between the ages of three to five years old. Eighty-five to 90 percent of a child's brain develops by age five! It is also thought that much of their personality is hard-wired at birth but can be manipulated to varying degrees in these first three to five years of life.

Observation: In 1906, Planned Parenthood was founded. It was founded on the idea that women should have the information and care they need to live strong, healthy lives and fulfill their dreams. Today, Planned Parenthood is a trusted healthcare provider, an informed educator, a passionate advocate, and a global partner helping similar organizations around the world. Planned Parenthood delivers vital reproductive health care, sex education, and information to millions of men, women, and young people worldwide. You would not realize these positive things about Planned Parenthood if you were to hear and listen to many of the disparaging things being said by many about this wonderful organization and all the good it does simply because there are those that don't believe the organization should be informing the public on birth control and abortion.

HUMANITY... "DON'T STOP YOUR HUMAN... EMBRACE IT!"®

- Compassionate, sympathetic, or generous behavior or disposition; the quality or state of being humane
- The human race; human beings collectively
- Humaneness; benevolence
- My definition, simply put, is "the way we treat each other humanly as a human being!"

Common sense wise, you would think there isn't much to discuss in this chapter, but I think many of man's problems start and end right here! I am sure we have all heard the statement, "treat others the way we want to be treated!" In theory, this sounds like the solution to all of man's problems dealing with "getting along"! But the reality is, we just can't seem to grasp that concept! It apparently just doesn't make common sense to us! What seems to make more sense to many of us is judging someone based on their race, nationality, religion, sex, sexual preference, etc. and treating them accordingly! We seem to miss an important point which is as individuals we are *all* different in the way we look, and as groups, we may seem different, but in reality, we are all the same in one and the most important aspect and that is we are *all* human! We may be different in many superficial areas like the language we speak, the color of our skin, the types of foods we eat, etc., but we are alike in the most important area, and again, that is we are *all* human!

Observation: Are people born evil? Are there evil babies? Evil definition: "Profoundly immoral and wicked." Based on this definition, it would be very difficult, if not impossible, to determine or label a baby immoral or wicked! Babies are very limited in their ability to fully express or display their personality or character. What is the magic age we can safely label someone evil? At that time, will we be able to say with a hundred-percent degree of confidence that they weren't born with a predisposition to be evil, but society or some other factor caused this evilness to occur?

Let's look at some of the most common areas where some seem to feel others are less human than they are and, as a result, frequently discriminates against them:

Race: Refers to a person's physical characteristics, such as bone structure and skin, hair, or eye color. Common sense wise, name a race that would say that they believe that *their* race is *inferior* to another race based on that definition. I would dare to guess and say that there probably isn't *any* race that would make that statement about their race! They may acknowledge that due to their race, they may be subject to some man-made disadvantages, but another race being superior to them isn't one of those disadvantages! I would agree that there are probably individuals within a particular race that might personally feel inferior to another race, but that would be a case of an individual with poor self-esteem or self-hatred! Are there races that feel that they are superior to other races? Yes! Absolutely! Many of these individuals within these races are well educated academically but are grossly lacking in common sense! Many of these "learned" academics also believe they have an intellectual advantage over other races in addition to the physical attributes previously mentioned above! Common sense and factually wise, it has been proven that if given the same tools and opportunities, no race has an advantage in any area over another race!

Gender: Either of the two sexes (male or female). It is common knowledge that there are some distinct differences between the two sexes. These differences are more distinct than the differences between races. Men are generally physically bigger and physically stronger than the average woman. Women can become pregnant and men can't! Men and women have different genitalia or sexual organs. Throughout human history in most cultures, the female has been designated and treated as the lesser of the two sexes! At this time in our human history, most people with a healthy degree of intelligence and common sense would agree that both sexes are equally important for the survival of the human race. Some humans are homosexual. They are sexually or romantically attracted to people of their sex. No one knows for sure what causes this. Some say it's a matter of choice, others say people are born this way. Common sense would say what truly matters is that they are human and deserve the same rights, benefits, and consideration as all other humans. Not all people feel that way and many choose to see them negatively and treat them accordingly.

Religion: A belief in and worship of a super being controlling power, especially a god or gods. It has been quite common to see other religions other than our own as different and less than and discriminate against them in employment, housing, business dealings, school, relationships in general!

In most cases, discrimination is passed on due to ignorance from generation to generation. It will probably continue unless the cycle of ignorance is broken.

> July 4–10, 2022 (social medial post): *What are some ways we can show more humanity toward each other?*
>
> Response: AT: *You and I both worked in a job where almost everyone who walked in the door had a problem. For instance, it was easy to believe that all military members have financial problems because those we saw did. However, we didn't see most people. We saw a small slice of the population, and it's easy to generalize to everyone else. I think that's what we see in the media (TV, magazines, newspapers, radio). They pick the outliers, the extreme ones, and focus on those people. It sells. It's sensational. It gets people riled up and emotional. Did I mention it sells? But what it also does is make it seem like that's the majority. I believe*

the majority are ordinary people with middle of the road ideals who are just going about their lives trying to do the best they can. The media shows us what they want us to see. Take photographs for example. They print the most unflattering photograph of the opposite side. You know those photographers took two thousand photos on burst, but they pick the worst one to make the other side look bad. It's all optics. As for examples of humanity, they are all around us. Every day. When you see someone waiting to turn on to a road, so you slow down and let them in. When an unknown kid trips on their untied shoelace in front of you and you bend down pick them, check and see if they are injured, and look around for their parents. When you sneeze and strangers say, "Bless you." When a stranger holds open a door. On Saturday, we were at Ace Hardware, and a man in the garden department collapsed outside and six strangers ran to help him, carrying him to the shade, calling 911, pouring water on him, trying to get him to talk, and the customers who were waiting in the checkout line just calmly waited (all the cashiers left to help) because they knew at that moment this man's life was the most important thing. Last week, my daughter woke up at 3:00 a.m. because she heard someone yelling, "Help me!" So she called 911 (turns out an elderly man had fallen out of his wheelchair). Signs of humanity are all around us. Just ordinary people going about their lives trying to do the best they can do. That doesn't sell.

My response: *AT, I agree with all you said about the acts of kindness and humanity that occur around us every day!*

Observation: *I do think the news media gets a bad rap in many cases for reporting so many negative or inhumane acts that occur daily! The definition of news is as follows: "Newly received or noteworthy information, especially about recent or important events." The definition of news media is as follows: "Those elements of the mass media that focus on delivering news to the general public or a target public." The acts of daily kindness and humanity you referenced should not be considered news but as an expectation, in my opinion! The following are analogies of how I think the news media generally works:*

- *A husband, for the last twenty years, treated his wife with a great degree of love, kindness, and humanity for twenty-nine out of thirty days in the month. On the thirtieth day, for the last twenty years, he severely beat her, showing no sign of love, kindness, or humanity! Which day or days should we be more concerned about?*
- *A father, for the last ten years, treated his eighteen-year-old daughter with a great degree of love, kindness, and humanity twenty-nine out of thirty days in the month! On the thirtieth day, for the last ten years, he raped her, showing no sign of love, kindness, or humanity! Which day or days should we be more concerned about?*

- *For the last ten years, twenty-nine out of thirty days a month, a police officer does not shoot and kill an unarmed Man of Color! On the thirtieth day, an unarmed Man of Color is shot multiple times in the back and killed! During that same time period, no person (not of color) was shot in the back and killed!*
- *For fifty-eight of fifty-nine times, there was a peaceful transfer of power between the two main political parties in the United States of America as a result of free and fair elections! On the fifty-ninth time, there was an attempt to not allow the peaceful transfer of power!*

I could go on but hopefully, the point has been made! There are certain expectations that we have that we consider to be normal and common sense. When those expectations have been violated, many of us might consider that newsworthy and would want to be informed of those violations!

Response: AT: *All true, but I combined two posts into one. The second half of my response was in response to your question of how we show humanity.*

The first half was in response to three people who want to erase history.

My response: *Oh, I am sorry! I have been known to miss a point, so I missed the point in the first half of your post about the three people who want to erase history. Who are the three people, and what is the history they are trying to erase?*

Response: AT: *Haha. I don't know. You mentioned three ladies in Phoenix who didn't want history taught.*

My response: *Oh! Lol! I am sorry! Girl, don't confuse me! I am very easily confused! Lol! That was in a different post! Lol! Yes, I agree that the vast majority of people would probably say that slavery was bad! I know I can be naive and see the positive side in most cases, but I am totally blown away that ANYONE who is NOT a racist can't see and won't say on national TV that slavery was a bad thing! So for me, I am grateful that the news media is informing me of this deep-seated racism that still exists even if it is a small percent of the population!*

Response: AT: *Lol. It was a different post. They were similar in my head...crazy things in the world and the seemingly lack of humanity. Haha. There are A LOT of things I can't believe people say and do in public, much less on a public platform (thank you, Jerry Springer). I just tell myself that's not the majority.*

LIFE

"A state of living characterized by the capacity for metabolism, growth, reaction to stimuli, and reproduction... The sequence of physical and mental experiences that make up the existence of an individual."

Life is a temporary gift given to us all who have been blessed with it! It will end for us all one day! Along with this temporary gift, we have been given a degree of choice, free choice, as to how we live our lives. We have been provided with an environment and the means to not just exist or survive but to flourish! Common sense wise, it is amazing to me how many of us do not recognize, realize, or understand what we have been given and therefore do not take full advantage of it to our benefit not realizing that this is a temporary gift, and it will be reclaimed at some future unknown moment! Instead, from our first breath of life, we come into the world kicking, crying, screaming, and complaining! Complaining sometimes throughout our entire lives about how bad things are for us and why we have had such bad luck! Never once do we take a look within ourselves and see and accept our choices, roles, and responsibilities in our predicaments! We see others who seem to be living happily stress- and problem-free lives, and we can't understand why that can't be us! Some people can see that we are having a "living" problem, and they reach out to us and try to offer us some guidance and suggestions on how we can improve our situation, but we can't seem to hear or understand what they are trying to tell us. Some of us are so unaware and ungrateful to what a great gift we have been blessed with that we contemplate and, in many cases, succeed at ending this great and wonderful gift by taking our own life or ending the lives of others! We have seen and heard of many famous and well-known people who have ended their own lives with no apparent logical reason as if there is a logical reason for taking your own life! Again, this is another instance where I am drawn to conclude that we are so hardwired in some cases that we will even end God's greatest gift to us all, our lives or someone else's life! If we are so illogical, ungrateful, and reckless as to contemplate and in many cases take our own lives or the lives of others, how can we be expected to realize and appreciate the blessings of just everyday life and living?

There are five universal truths of the life cycle of man. I initially thought there were three—life, death, and the in-between, or more commonly referred to as living. But after much thought, I realized there are two more—the before life and the afterlife, death. These truths are not dependent on one's gender, race, or any other trait or traits that render one human. The only universal truth we truly know about the life cycle and have a degree of control over is the in-between or living. There doesn't seem to be much thought, discussion, or interest about the before life, except maybe the question of when does life begin. There are many thoughts, opinions, and much discussion about what happens in the afterlife, referred to as death. No one truly knows about the before life or after death. Many in religious circles claim to know about after death. None of these thoughts or claims of the after death have been verified or are even verifiable by man.

Many of us base our in-between or living on our thoughts about after death, even though we don't truly know what happens in after death. Living our lives or the in-between based on what we know and personally experience would seem to make more common sense than basing it on a place called heaven (the abode of God and angels and the good after death, depicted as being above the sky) or hell (a spiritual realm of evil and suffering traditionally depicted as a place of perpetual fire beneath the earth where the wicked are punished after death).

July 11–17, 2022 (social medial post): Last week's discussion was on humanity. This week, Walter Kamau Bell, an American stand-up comic and television host on CNN, did a series on critical race theories. He interviewed three women in Phoenix, Arizona, and asked them if it would be okay if a teacher told their students that slavery was bad. He asked another lady if she thought slavery was bad. If you saw the series, you heard their answers. For those of you that didn't see the series, they all said no! They did not feel that teachers should tell their students that slavery was bad, and one lady said she didn't even think it was bad! There is a movement in this country today to not even teach about slavery in school! Is this where humanity is in the United States of America today? We just ignore our past and present inhumanity and just act like it never happened and doesn't exist? For those of you that say we shouldn't dwell on it, I agree, but it is part of our country's history, and shouldn't our kids know all our country's history—the good, the bad, and the ugly?

This week's discussion topic is life; technical definition is "A state of living characterized by the capacity for metabolism, growth, reaction to stimuli, and reproduction... The sequence of physical and mental experiences that make up the existence of an individual."

Life is a temporary gift given to us all who have been blessed with it! It will end for us all one day! Along with this temporary gift, we have been given a degree of choice, free choice, as to how we live our lives. We have been provided with an environment and the means to not just exist or survive but to flourish! Common sense wise, it is amazing to me how many of us do not recognize, realize, or understand what we have been given and therefore take full advantage of it to our benefit not realizing that this is a temporary gift, and it will be reclaimed at some future unknown moment! Instead, from our first breath of life, we come into the world kicking, crying, screaming, and complaining! Complaining sometimes throughout our entire lives about how bad things are and why we have had such bad luck! Never once do we look within ourselves and see and accept our choices, roles, and responsibilities in our predicaments! We see others who seem to be living happy stress- and problem-free lives, and we can't understand why that can't be us! Some people can see that we are having a "living" problem, and they reach out to us and try to offer us some guidance and suggestions on how we can improve our situation, but we can't seem to hear or understand what they are trying to tell us. Some of us are so unaware and ungrateful for what a great gift we have been blessed with that we contemplate and, in many cases, succeed at ending this great and wonderful gift by taking our own life or ending the lives of others! We have seen and heard of many famous and well-known people who have ended their own lives with no apparent logical reason as if there is a logical reason for taking your own life! Again, this is another instance where I am drawn to conclude that we are so hardwired in some cases that we will even end God's greatest gift to us all, our lives or someone else's life! If we are so illogical, ungrateful, and reckless as to contemplate and in many cases take our own lives or the lives of others, how can we be expected to realize and appreciate the blessings of just everyday life and living?

Response: LC: *Agree. A study focusing on negativity showed the more a person complains, the more it becomes habit. The deeper the habit, the less they are capable of being positive. On the flip side, people seeking treatment for depression are encouraged to donate time to help others. Especially after a loss, it gives them something to do to see a positive result in another's life. In turn bringing positivity back into their own. As for the rest? I can't condone erasing history. Even the worst parts need to be told and remembered. So I hope we are never tempted to be that awful again.*

VALUES

They are core beliefs that support and guide our decision-making and behaviors. Values are basic and fundamental beliefs that guide or motivate attitudes or actions. Many of our day-to-day decisions are based on our values. We are often most comfortable, content, and without internal conflict when we can stick to our values. We can feel extremely uncomfortable and unhappy when we are not able to act according to our values. This discomfort can take on many forms, from anger to anxiety, and can feel confusing if we're not aware of where it's coming from! There are many times our values and our common sense conflict with each other. Values tend to be stable but aren't necessarily fixed. Values tend to grow and change as we grow and change. Living close to our values is ideal but not always possible. There will be people and situations in life where we feel a need to compromise our values or fight to stick by them. There is a difference between values and things we value! Our values are things that can't be taken from us! Things we value can be taken from us! For example, kindness is a value of mine. No one can take that from me. Money, on the other hand, is something I value, but it can be taken from me! "A person's principles or standards of behavior; one's judgment of what is important in life!"

> July 18–24, 2022 (social medial post): Observation: *On last week's topic on life, many of us base our in-between or living on our thoughts about after death, even though we don't truly know what happens after death. Living our lives or the in-between based on what we know and personally experience*

would seem to make more common sense than basing it on a place called heaven (the abode of God and angels and the good after death, depicted as being above the sky) or hell (a spiritual realm of evil and suffering traditionally depicted as a place of perpetual fire beneath the earth where the wicked are punished after death).

The two most selfish acts committed by man are murder, the unlawful premeditated killing of one human being by another, and suicide, death caused by injuring oneself with the intent to die! I won't claim to know what causes an individual to commit either of these acts, but both acts leave many victims in their wake! The suicide victims themselves are no longer with us, so the possible reasons for this act will never be verified...

This week's discussion topic is values! Values are core beliefs that support and guide our decision-making and behaviors. Values are basic and fundamental beliefs that guide or motivate attitudes or actions. Many of our day-to-day decisions are based on our values. We are often most comfortable, content, and without internal conflict when we can stick to our values. We can feel extremely uncomfortable and unhappy when we are not able to act according to our values. Thoughts on values?

Response: MAR: *From a biblical point on what I believe, Bible has always been my guide for eternity. The price of what Jesus Christ did, died and rose again for our sins, is a daily crucifying our flesh. We are not saved by our works, only from Acts 2:38, this scripture is for today. For the suicide part is a harder point to* make. *But because you can't ask for forgiveness, I believe you're not in heaven. When I pray on a daily basis, I ask for forgiveness of my iniquity and transgressions. So when I go to sleep and if I die, my sins are forgiven.*

My response: *From a biblical point, we are talking about one's faith! I do not question one's faith... It is personal to that person and should not be questioned or judged by others...*

Response: MAR: *When death is done and over, what we do on earth for our lives make it worth living in obedience to the Word of God. Yes, we all make mistakes but living a holy and righteous life is worth to make heaven.*

My response: *Again, we are talking about one's faith and belief, and it shouldn't be questioned or judged by others...*

Response: MAR: *You're right, but one day, I will give account if I don't share the truth. It's not about judging but the right judgment is biblical.*

Response: MAR: *I can't hold the truth back even if it upsets people. I only want to see people come to the knowledge of the TRUTH OF GOD with Pastor Gino Jennings. His preaching is all Bible.*

My response: *Again, that is your personal belief and should not be questioned...*

Response: MAR: *Okay, bro, I remember how you are. No argument from me. I made my humble point of truth.*

My response: *Again, that is your personal opinion, and you have a right to that, and I will not question that, so there is no argument on my part...*

Response: LC: *I agree completely. Call it what you will: morals, principles, values, etc. If people are only not sinning out of fear of the afterlife, they still don't get it. It is more than following ten rules to achieve a prize. I am to walk a path closest to what God wants. If I were to spend my time fantasizing about adultery but never physically following through, am I any less immoral? No. I would be just as much a sinner. If I were to go to church every single week but spend my other six days and twenty-three hours condemning others for their sins or not living a righteous enough life, would I be any less immoral? No. I choose to do my best to follow a moral path not because of fear of consequences in the afterlife but because of who I want to be in this life.*

My response: *Well said, LC.*

July 23, 2022 (social medial post): Update: *There will be people and situations in life where we feel a need to compromise our values or fight to stick by them. There is a difference between values and things we value! Our values are things that can't be taken from us! Things we value can be taken from us! For example, kindness is a value of mine. No one can take that from me. Money, on the other hand, is something I value, but it can be taken from me! As stated previously, our values have a tendency to grow and change as we grow and change!*

Response: GO: *Excellent observation! Other things that have value but can't be taken are character, morality, ethics, integrity, and so forth.*

My response: *I find it to be very curious that so many people today are so willing to give up those things you mentioned—like character, morality, ethics, integrity, and so forth—to others so freely for no apparent reason! Any thoughts on why this occurs?*

Response: SW: *GO, just to add to this as a personal observation but I think culture today has poor value for life. When you don't value life, those other things don't matter as much. Or maybe it's a perceived loss of value of life due to social media, video games, ease of communication without consequence.*

Response: JW: *Very well said!*

Response: MS: *Totally agree!*

Response: GO: *First the traits I mentioned are taught. If a person wasn't taught "don't lie, don't cheat, don't steal," etc. Then there is nothing to give up.*

Second some people, perhaps many people, will trade their values for a perceived gain. For example, I had a discussion with a Trump supporter during the past election who freely acknowledged that Trump lacked most of the character traits we look for in a human being. But because Trump ran the country well (in his opinion) he was willing to accept the flaws.

Finally, people don't all value the same things. I place a very high value on keeping one's word, honesty, compassion and so forth. Others may not. So, it is relatively easy to give up what one doesn't value in exchange for something that holds more value to that person.

Response: JG: *Powerful.*

Response: JR: *Integrity, honor, others before self without sacrificing you, dedication, and*

> *understanding failure is not fatality, just opportunity to learn.*
>
> My response: *The world would be a much better place if more of us sought and applied those qualities…*
>
> Response: DB: *Well said!*
>
> Response: NS: *Comments right on point.*

Observation: Common sense is more stable and consistent than values. As stated above, values tend to grow and change as we grow and change.

MONEY/FINANCES

I will admit right off, knowledge of financial management has never been one of my strongest qualities or abilities, but I must say, my wife and I have learned a few commonsense basics about money and financial management, and we have done fairly well financially!

My first very simple lesson about money and finances came from my mother whose formal education didn't go beyond the sixth grade. She simply said, "Son, there are going to be many things you will want in life that will cost money! So get it in your mind that you will have to work for those things! People aren't just going to just give you money without wanting something in return!" That simple lesson has stuck with me my whole life! My wife and I have worked our whole adult lives, and we are not what I would call financially rich, but we are finically secure to the point where money is not an issue we have to deal with in our lives. Growing up, I never thought I would ever be able to utter those words, but it is true! The following are some simple commonsense financial principles we have lived by:

- Accept that you will probably have to work a large part of your adult life if you don't come from a family with money or you can't make a large sum of money in a relatively short period of time.
- Find a job and career you enjoy and can grow in and stick with.
- Earn more money monthly than your monthly expenses. Save and invest the excess.
- Work together with your partner if you have one, financial goals should be closely aligned.

- Save and invest toward financial stability and retirement. Have more than one savings account.
  - Retirement/investment
  - Education saving
  - Vacation saving
  - Discretionary fund
  - Emergency saving
  - Don't have separate or "secret" accounts
- Don't waste money on unnecessary items like smoking, drinking, gambling, overly expensive cars, clothes, jewelry, overly expensive houses, etc.
- Avoid purchasing on credit cards; if you do, pay off at the end of the month.
- Reward yourself for your hard work accordingly.
- Work toward purchasing a home instead of renting.
- Refrain from the impulse of buying a new car as soon as your old car purchased four years ago is paid off.
- Don't be a victim of get-rich-quick schemes.
- Teach your kids the basics of finances and money management early; give them a reasonable allowance for weekly chores completed and have them open a savings account.

EVERYDAY VIOLATORS OF THE RULES OF COMMON SENSE

If the following examples of common everyday violators of the rules of common sense don't have you questioning the average person's capacity, or lack thereof, for common sense, I am sure nothing will!

Driving: The maximum posted street legal speed limit in the United States is eighty-five miles per hour.

- Speedometers are registered to go between 140 through 300 miles per hour on street-legal motor vehicles sold in the US.
- Drivers on freeways will typically drive fifteen to twenty miles per hour over the posted speed limit, still falling well short of the 140–300 miles per hour registered on speedometers, so why is there 140–300 miles per hour on street-legal motor vehicles in the US?
- Drivers may receive tickets for impeding the flow of traffic if they are going the posted speed limit, but the other traffic that is flowing faster than the posted speed limit may not receive a ticket.
- Many drivers speed up to prevent other drivers from changing lanes and getting in front of them when they see other drivers put their turn signals on to change lanes. Because this is a well-known practice, many drivers will not use turn signals when changing lanes thereby angering the very drivers that would not allow them to change lanes and merge in front of them anyway if they had used their turn signals! Since this is common knowledge to most drivers

that aren't babies or those with mental challenges, is this a form of common sense?
- Many drivers will come to a complete stop to change lanes on a freeway where traffic is traveling sixty-five through eighty-five miles per hour to make their exit instead of taking the next exit. Many of these drivers are the same drivers who slow down or stop when they see an accident on the freeway, even when it is on the other side of the freeway! This explains why you at times have to come to a crawl or complete stop on the freeway, and you are wondering what the cause was of this sudden and unexplained phenomenon.
- Drivers who violate the law and commonsense rule of traveling on the left when the traffic is traveling faster and, in many cases, much faster, to their right.
- It is quite common to see drivers stop in the crosswalk at red lights. Do they not realize it will be difficult for pedestrians to utilize the crosswalk if they are blocking it or for fellow drivers wanting to turn right on red to see around them for traffic coming from their left?
- General road rage
- Texting and talking on the phone
- Driving under the influence of prescription drugs when instructions and common sense say not to:
  - Using illegal drugs
  - Driving while intoxicated
  - Driving without an operator's license, registration, or insurance

Addictions: Websters defines addictions as a compulsive, chronic, physiological, or psychological need for a habit-forming substance, behavior, or activity having harmful physical, psychological, or social effects and typically causing well-defined symptoms (such as anxiety, irritability, tremors, or nausea) upon withdrawal or abstinence… the state of being addicted! Most addicted individuals do not believe they are addicted. Studies show that there are addictive genes that put some people more at risk for addictions. Some of the most common addictions are:

- *Substance abuse:* For a definition, substance abuse is the overindulgence or dependence on an addictive substance, especially alcohol or drugs! As a prior substance abuse counselor, it was my experience that the vast majority of people I counseled didn't see themselves as addicted or substance abusers! I will not attempt to counsel anyone on the well-known and well-advertised negative consequences and risks associated with substance abuse. But I will again remind you of the definition of common sense, "knowledge that should be common to most everyone except babies and those that have mental challenges!"

Observation: Today in the US, more than seven million people suffer from an illicit drug disorder, and one in four deaths results from illicit drug use. More deaths, illnesses, and disabilities are associated with drug abuse than any other preventable health condition. People suffering from drug and alcohol addiction also have a higher risk of unintentional injuries, accidents, and domestic violence incidents. So knowing all these negative consequences, what would cause someone to start using addictive substances in the first place?

- *Smokers:* The following are some of the warnings that are printed on cigarette boxes and packs and people still start and continue smoking:
  - Smoking is highly addictive, don't start.
  - Smoking harms nearly every organ in the body.
  - Smoking clogs the arteries and causes heart attacks and strokes.
  - Smoking causes fatal lung cancer.
  - Smokers die younger.
  - Smoking can cause a slow and painful death.
  - Smoking kills.

Observation: Are you aware of any other product where the producers, manufacturers, or sellers of the product market or advertise their product in such a way as to inform you of its dangers if used and the only thing that appears to affect sales is a price increase? When the price of cigarettes goes up, sales decrease slightly. The average smoker knows or has known someone who has or has had complications resulting from smoking, but yet they start and continue anyway! Many smokers continue to smoke even after a stroke or heart attack, many times after multiple occurrences. The main reason people continue to smoke: *ADDICTION!* The younger you are when you begin smoking, the more likely you are to become addicted to nicotine.

The following are some of the common reasons people say they smoke:

- Stress relief
- Perks me up
- Pleasant and relaxing
- Takes my mind off worrying
- Social situations
- Lose weight
- Habit
- Addicted

The following are reasons not to smoke:

- Smoking is the number one cause of lung cancer…increases the chances of developing lung cancer by 30 percent
- Doubles your chances of getting tuberculosis
- Twenty percent of smokers will develop heart disease
- Thirty to 40 percent more likely to develop type 2 diabetes
- Increases risk for liver cancer
- Causes erectile dysfunction
- Increases the risk of cataracts and glaucoma
- Increases the risk of developing rheumatoid arthritis
- Smokers are more likely to die from colorectal cancer

DNA... HARDWIRED...

- Smokers can lose at least ten years of their life
- Makes it more likely to have a stroke
- Smoking is the number one reason for bladder cancer
- The risk of cervical cancer doubles for women who smoke
- Smoking makes your skin look older and discolors your fingernails and teeth
- Secondhand smoke is dangerous to your family and others
- Life insurance rates are 20 to 30 percent lower for nonsmokers
- Approximately 60 percent of nonsmokers will not date smokers

There are many more negative side effects, but if this and the warnings written on cigarette packing isn't enough to convince one to stop or not to start smoking, what is?

Food addiction: Simply put, food addiction is a loss of control overeating behaviors. It is thought that anyone can develop an addiction to food. People who are overexposed at a young age and those who use food to cope with stress or change their mood are at an even higher risk of food addiction. If you haven't noticed or weren't aware, there are more obese people in the world today than, let's say, forty to fifty years ago. Why is this? Some say that we just practice less self-control over overeating than in the past. This is true, but is it completely our fault, and are we to blame? Consider the fact that food companies have invested heavily in developing food products that use more sugar today than in the past to bypass our natural appetite control mechanisms. They have packaged and promoted these products to break down our defenses, including through the use of subliminal scents. Food companies employ an army of food scientists and psychologists to trick us into eating more than we need while their advertisers use the latest techniques to overcome our resistance. They spend billions on overriding our willpower and then blame us for not exercising better willpower. Just as jobless people are blamed for unemployment and indebted people are blamed for impossible housing costs, fat people are blamed for a societal problem. Yes, willpower and control need to be exercised by those that are overweight, but control needs to also be exerted over those who have discovered our weaknesses and ruthlessly exploit those weaknesses!

> August 15–21, 2022 (social medial post): *This week's discussion topic is what are your thoughts on people who drive under the influence of prescription drugs, alcohol, and illegal drugs?*
>
> Response: AT: *Scary, selfish, dangerous, irresponsible, and if caught should be punished. I agree it's a disease. I also agree that many people don't know they're sick and those that do don't realize how to get treatment. Also, it's usually the impaired brain that's deciding to get behind the wheel. Once, during FTAC (First Term Airmen Course) there at Luke, I overhead a young lady tell the ADAPT (US Air Force Alcohol and Drug Abuse Treatment Program) guy that she can still drive after four drinks… She was impaired at five but four was okay. I told her I was going to give her my number and every time she got behind the wheel to call me so I could make sure I wasn't on the road. Regardless, a decision was made that very first time to take that drug/drink. Unfortunately, irresponsible and dangerous decisions usually lead to more irresponsible and dangerous decisions…and then innocent people pay the price.*
>
> August 22–28, 2022 (social medial post): *The consensus on last week's discussion of driving under the influence of prescription drugs, alcohol, and illegal drugs was that there was no reasonable excuse for doing it! I agree that we should strive toward preventing ourselves and*

others from driving while impaired! A significant problem with this thought process is that once a person is impaired, their judgment is also impaired, and they will not think rationally and will probably drive. I fear that as long as there are mind-altering substances, easy access to them, and motor vehicles, there will be people who will drive while impaired, and many innocent people will suffer the consequences...

This week's discussion topic is your thoughts on additions in general. Websters defines additions as a compulsive, chronic, physiological, or psychological need for a habit-forming substance, behavior, or activity having harmful physical, psychological, or social effects and typically causing well-defined symptoms (such as anxiety, irritability, tremors, or nausea) upon withdrawal or abstinence... The state of being addicted. So what are your thoughts on additions, legal and illegal?

My response: *I suspect people don't set out to become addicted. Like many things, we decide to try different addictive substances for many different reasons and end up addicted physiologically and or psychologically. I, like you, find it confusing why anyone would start using these substances knowing the problems it has caused to many others! I also suspect that if there was an easy and effective preventive process or cure, the problem would not exist. This is another one of those many life situations that drive me to try and figure out why we behave the way we do many times. I appreciate your feedback because it gives me more to consider...*

Response: AT: *I agree with you... No one sets out to become an addict. I think people feel they're* an exception. It won't happen to them. They can control it. Etc. Etc. People feel invincible. Which also leads people to drive too fast (a previous conversation). Why do people think they are invincible? What common sense does that make? It's like gambling…sometimes you lose, but sometimes you don't.

My response: *Yes, I agree with the attitude of it won't happen to me and that I am invincible probably have a lot to do with people taking these risks. I have a theory that many of these people weren't taught to have a healthy degree of fear growing up! I think without a certain degree of fear, it is difficult to have respect and caution for things that might hurt us.*

Response: LC: *Agreed.*

Observation: After much research on addictions and having been a substance abuse counselor for many years myself, I have concluded that there is something at work that goes far beyond the concept of common sense when trying to explain and understand addictions! I am leaning more toward one's DNA or one being hardwired and more predisposed to becoming addicted rather than a lack of common sense! I must admit, this has been one of the most difficult areas to cover in this book. I am not presently addicted, nor have I ever been, but I could feel the hopelessness and helplessness the average addicted individual must feel trying to fight their demon! I strongly recommend and encourage those that may be a victim of some form of addiction to please seek professional help! It appears to be the most promising solution! Many do overcome many of these addictions on their own but not before paying a heavy price in many cases! For those may be friends, family, or loved ones of the addicted, please understand that if they had control over their condition, believe me, they would gladly exercise that control! They need your support and understanding, not your judgment!

LIFE'S LESSONS...
SHITTY THOUGHTS

- Wise men aren't truly any wiser than the average man... They just exercise a healthy dose of common sense and more consistently.
- Life can be hard... It will be harder if you are stupid.
- Consider the possibility that there are those that appear to lack common sense but, in reality, are mentally challenged and aren't aware of it.
- Unreasonable and illogical people should not be expected to be reasonable and logical... After all, they are unreasonable and illogical.
- Your vision of a situation isn't always as clear to others as it is as clear to you... You are looking through different lenses with different filters.
- You may have a right to say or do a thing, but it doesn't mean or make you or that thing right.
- Saying it is so does not thereby make it so.
- Telling a lie does not make it true... It is still a lie.
- If you eat fattening and unhealthy foods, you will be fat, unhealthy, unattractive, and probably alone...or with someone who thinks the way you do about their health and appearance.
- Smoking, drinking, drugging, and other forms of unhealthy risky behaviors are risky and unhealthy and often lead to health problems and ultimately early death.
- If you don't brush and floss your teeth daily, see the dentist periodically; your teeth will decay, be very unattractive, and will eventually be lost.

- A positive attitude and positive behavior tend to lead to a positive lifestyle and outcome.
- A negative attitude and negative behavior tend to lead to a negative lifestyle and outcome.
- I will *not* help you the way *you* want me to help you…Your way is *not working*.
- A risky lifestyle is risky and full of risk and will likely lead to danger, failure, or loss.
- Your lifestyle often defines you… Changes in one's life don't usually occur without a lifestyle change.
- There is no such thing as true unconditional love…even God has conditions for you to enter heaven.
- Some people will treat you meanly and unkind no matter how kind you are and how good you treat them… There are mean and unkind people… It's their nature.
- Treating people the way you want them to treat you does not guarantee they will treat you the way you want them to treat you…but the odds are better.
- There are givers and takers, users and the used, determine who you are and stay in your lane… The world's balance and survival depend on it…
- If you expect positive changes to occur in your life, you must make positive changes and decisions in your life.
- Your experiences and situations in life are YOUR experiences and situations.
- Don't expect others to live in your fantasy if it is not theirs also.
- Do not live in others' fantasies unless they are yours also.
- Having money gives you a better chance of being happy in life than not having money, my response to those who say, "money can't make you happy."
- If I see you lie to someone else, common sense tells me others will see you lie to me.
- If you find many different people are telling you the same things about yourself, consider they may be true.
- Some say work hard and play hard, I say don't…it's too hard.

DNA... HARDWIRED...

- Many say along life's journey, "work hard, save, retire, and then enjoy..." I prefer to enjoy life's journey along the way... We don't know when the journey will end, and I prefer others not to enjoy the fruits of my labor.
- If you live long enough, your outside beauty will fade... Inside ugliness tends to grow and flourish with age and is usually lifelong.
- There will be people who don't like you...don't you be one of them
- Ladies, if you are sexy and attractive and dress very sexy or provocatively in public places like the gym, parks, malls, grocery stores, etc., men will look, stare, and possibly comment inappropriately.
- Ladies, if you are unattractive and dress very sexy or provocatively in public places like the gym, parks, malls, grocery stores, etc., men will look, stare, and possibly comment inappropriately.
- One day we *all* will die... In the meantime, live... "Don't stop your human...embrace it!"

CLOSING THOUGHTS

There is a god...sometimes referred to as God, Jesus, a superior being, Creator, Higher Power, the Supreme, the Almighty, Allah, Father in Heaven, Heavenly Father, Jehovah, King of Kings, Lord of Lords, Yahweh, Buddha, Krishna, Shiva, Wakan Taka, and there are many more references. The main point of all these names or descriptions is that man, the human race, all life, were created by some superior being or beings. There are many thoughts, beliefs, theories as to who this superior being is and how they created all life, but there is a common agreement among most people that all life just doesn't appear one day from nothing, out of nowhere, with no defined purpose.

There are those that do not believe in a god, a creator, or a higher power. I have done much research to try and determine what these nonbelievers do believe in as far as where life did come from or how life originated. I have not found a consistent explanation. Many simply say they don't know or they don't think about it... They just don't believe there is a god or creator. It appears that the reason many nonbelievers have a problem with the existence of a god is due to religion being associated with God. There are so many religions and gods that I can understand how some people might prefer not to get involved in trying to figure out who the real god and true religion is! As I stated previously, I do believe there is a god or creator, but I don't have any clue as to what that is or what it looks like, so I don't follow any religion. In reality, believers don't have any more factual evidence or proof that there is a god than the nonbelievers have that there isn't! What I do have is the following facts about life that lead me to believe that life is far too complicated to have just happened by accident:

- It is believed that all life shares at least some DNA.
- Humans and chimpanzees are 99.9 percent identical in their DNA.
- Humans are 99.9 percent identical to the person sitting next to us.
- Ninety percent of the genes in the Abyssinian domestic cat are similar to humans.
- Domestic cattle share about 80 percent of their DNA with humans.
- Genetics between chickens and humans is 60 percent.
- Humans share 60 percent of their DNA with bananas.
- When it comes to noncoding genes, mice are 50 percent similar to humans.
- All living things have a body of some kind and are made of at least one cell.
- All living things consume food for energy and growth.
- All life reproduces in some way.
- All life eventually dies.

I stated at the beginning of this book that I didn't believe that this book would change many people's minds on common sense in a meaningful way. I was hoping I was wrong, but I am even more convinced now after conducting much research and interviewing many people and getting their feedback and their ideas on some areas dealing with common sense. I believe I was right then, and I am still right now, that people's minds would not be changed in a meaningful way on common sense after writing this book! It is somewhat reassuring though, in a twisted sort of way; I have concluded that people don't truly have a whole lot of control over many of the decisions they make that might call their common sense into question. I hope that people don't think I am attempting to make or give excuses to those who don't always exercise a reasonable degree of common sense when required, but the hardwired effect on our psychological makeup and mental disorders are very real and are very powerful forces, especially when you don't realize or accept that they exist! I must admit that there were many times in researching and writing this book that I became very saddened. Saddened with where we appear to be at this time in our human evolution and development. We are at a time where human life itself doesn't appear to hold the value it used to hold in years gone by. We are at a time where money, power, and fame are the new priorities and at an all-time high in value! People will lie, cheat, and do whatever it takes to acquire and maintain those things.

Did you take me up on my challenge at the beginning of the book to work on an area in your life to change? How did you do? As human beings, we are hardwired in so many areas that it is very difficult common sense wise to overcome this condition. The best we can do is to attempt to recognize some of these hardwired areas, and if they are affecting our lives in negative ways, do what we can to effect some positive change. It will also be helpful to realize and understand the effects of the hardwired effects on others in our lives and how that could be affecting our relationships with them. Remember, seeking professional help is always a smart option and course of action and indicates good common sense! I will leave you with the following formula which might help you navigate life's journey and many challenges; OUTLOOK + PLAN + ACTION = OUTCOME

"Don't Stop Your Human... Embrace it! ®

ABOUT THE AUTHOR

James Knuckles was born and raised in Pittsburgh, Pennsylvania. He came from a very poor background and was raised by his mother as a single parent, but she raised him and his sister in such a way that he never felt the full effects of their poverty. He graduated from high school during the Vietnam era in 1967. He joined the United States Air Force in 1967, immediately after graduating from high school in an attempt to avoid being drafted into the army and sent to Vietnam. He was in the air force for less than a year and was sent to Nha Trang, Vietnam, in 1968 for a year. His goal was to serve in the air force for four years and then get out.

Twenty years and six months later, he retired from the air force. While serving in the air force, he was an aircraft mechanic for the first half of his career. The second half of his career, he was a substance abuse counselor. Growing up in the environment and the conditions he grew up in, he could never have imagined being able to attain and excel in either of those careers, but he did!

After retiring from the air force after a successful twenty-year career, he rejoined the air force as a Department of the Air Force civilian! He served thirty-four years with the air force as a Department of Defense civilian, assisting military members, families, and leadership with programs and services to strengthen communities, encourage self-sufficiency, enhance mission readiness, and ease adaptation to the military way of life. His service to his country has been one of the most rewarding experiences he has had the pleasure of enjoying in life!